About the Author

JESSICA GRIBETZ lives in New York City with her
husband and four daughters.

WISE WORDS

*Jewish Thoughts and Stories
Through the Ages*

COMPILED BY
JESSICA GRIBETZ

Quill

An Imprint of HarperCollins*Publishers*

When I was approaching my twelfth birthday, my father, who felt that the most important part of education took place outside the classroom, asked me to analyze a section of the Talmud in honor of my bat mitzvah at a time when it was unheard of for an Orthodox girl to do anything scholarly for her bat mitzvah. As an extremely social adolescent as well as a perennial postponer, I kept putting off the project and never did complete it. My father died that year, three months after my twelfth birthday. It is in his honor and memory that I completed this project and offer *Wise Words*.

CONTENTS

INTRODUCTION

*T*HERE IS A STORY about a great Hasidic rabbi, Rabbi Zisye, who was on his deathbed surrounded by his family and students. Suddenly he began to cry. The students asked him why he was crying. He replied that he was thinking of his appearance before the heavenly court and how he would justify his life. "If I am asked," he told them, " 'Why were you not as great as Abraham?' I will have an easy answer. 'I was not born with Abraham's intellectual abilities.' If I am asked, 'Rabbi, why were you not as great as Moses?' I will also have an easy answer. 'I was not born with his leadership abilities.' But if I am asked, 'Why were you not as great as Zisye could have been?' for that I will have no answer." My husband likes to tell this story to our children when they feel overwhelmed by the demands of a very competitive world.

My husband's teacher used this story to personalize a beautiful passage in Deuteronomy in which Moses exhorts his people to stay faithful to their traditions. "Because this commandment which I command thee this day is not too hard for thee, neither is it far off. It is not in heaven that you should say who will go up to heaven and bring it unto us and make us hear it that we may do it . . . neither is it beyond the sea . . . but the word is close

unto thee in thy mouth and in thy heart that thee may do it."
(30:11–13)

The values and lessons we derive from the Torah, from its wealth of commentary, and from our Jewish legends and parables are the foundation of our culture, as vitally relevant to our lives now as to generations past. They speak to each of us, whether we have the abilities of an Abraham or Moses, or just want to be the best Zisye we can be.

We have been called "Am Hasefer," "The People of the Book." From our passion for that book, the Torah, has come over thousands of years an ever-expanding literature that deals with every aspect of the human condition. That literature is both religious and secular, fiction and nonfiction. It has been molded by our historical experience and its writers over the centuries have defined a uniquely Jewish viewpoint. Martin Buber says in *Israel and the World*

> We Jews are a community based on memory. A common memory has kept us together and enabled us to survive. This does not mean that we based our life on any one particular past, even on the loftiest of pasts; it simply means that one generation passed on to the next a memory which gained in scope—for new destiny and new emotional life were constantly accruing to it—and which realized itself in a way we can call organic. This expanding memory was more than a spiritual motif; it was a power which sustained, fed, and quickened Jewish existence itself.

In Judaism there are two words for tradition—*kabalah* (not to be confused with the mystical book of Kabbalah) and *masoret*. Kabalah is what we receive and Masoret is what we transmit. Each generation has received from the previous generation and then has added to and modified what it received and then, keeping the kernel of eternal truth, has passed it on to the next generation.

Wise Words is a very small gleaning from the huge harvest of Jewish memories that has molded us as a people. It is meant to share the teaching and values of this very ancient people. And I hope that it will inspire in the reader the same love of Judaism and its values that I inherited from my parents and teachers and they from theirs in an unbroken chain begun by our biblical fathers and mothers.

Many of the quotations in *Wise Words* are proverbs and aphorisms from biblical writings, the Talmud, and contemporary writers. Others are parables, legends, and mystical meditations that speak of Jewish spirituality and philosophy. Still others are reminiscences of Jewish thinkers and artists on their childhoods and on their craft, with some musings on life in general. I have included excerpts from short stories as well as poetry wherever I could and I have intentionally selected a predominance of women's voices, as well as a separate section on women, in order to allow the reader to appreciate some of these often neglected voices as well as to raise some of the issues women have faced in Judaism for generations. I have divided the book into sections following the natural life-cycle themes—life, death, family, holidays, friendship, love, and marriage. I have also included quotations from the Jewish perspective on charity, ethics, food, nature, health, art, the Holocaust, and Israel—themes that are important to us in our daily lives both as Jews and as members of our communities.

In a seventh grade Talmud class, in a small day school on Long Island, I learned a passage that made a lasting impression on me. "Whoever reports a saying in the name of its originator brings the world toward redemption." (*Ethics of the Fathers* 6:6) On the surface, this may seem like a homiletic exaggeration of "give credit where credit is due," but like most talmudic sayings, it contains a more profound truth and is based on Jewish historical experience. The Book of Esther relates how Haman hoped to convince King Ahasvarus to issue an edict that would lead to the destruction of the Jewish community of Persia. Previously, Mordechai, Esther's uncle, had uncovered a conspiracy that two of the king's guards were plotting to kill the king. Mordechai related this to Queen Esther, who passed the information to the king and the plot was aborted. Esther gave the credit to Mordechai and it was duly recorded in the chronicles of the land. Months later, the book relates that the king was unable to sleep and asked that the chronicles be read to him. He noted that Mordechai had never been repaid for saving his life. Subsequent events led to Mordechai's rise to power and Haman's downfall. Had Esther not given due credit to Mordechai, the entire Jewish community of Persia might have been destroyed. Most of us undoubtedly lead more mundane lives than Esther and Mordechai and our ability to alter the course of world events is more limited, but the lesson is that since we cannot know what lies ahead—what may seem to us a minor omission, may in fact have profound consequences.

In this vein, I gratefully give credit to Francine Klagsbrun, Rabbi Joseph Telushkin, Noah Ben-Shea, Nathan Ausubel, Leo Rosten, and Alfred Kolatch for their scholarly collections of quotations and stories that have enriched my life and provided much valuable source material for this book. To my editor, Claire Wachtel, for all her support. To my husband, Allen, and my friends Holly Wertheimer and Judy Graubart for their invaluable help and insights on the book. To Dana Barak for her wonderful suggestions of Hebrew poets, to Ellen Pall and our shared love of Marcel Proust, to Abba for his huge library—thank goodness he put his name in his books—to Michael Oren for suggestions for the Israel section, to Tracy Quinn for her assistance on permissions; and to my brother-in-law, Jonathan, for E-mail and Philo, to Dorothy Glasser for the title, and to all those friends and family members who put up with a year of my speaking "in quote." While the Jewish Theological Seminary provided a wealth of material, I loved this project because I rediscovered the treasures of my own bookshelves. I also could not have managed without the weekly shopping bags of cookbooks and Russian and Yiddish stories that Judy schlepped uptown and, of course, my children, who regularly filled their backpacks with my requests from the Ramaz School library.

A memory has frequently crossed my mind since I first sat down to write this book. I have four daughters and they all attend the Ramaz School in New York City, a Jewish day school. Last year, my youngest daughters, Anna and Kate, were singing with their third grade class in the annual Zimriah, a concert presented by the lower school. The theme of the evening was Jerusalem in honor of Israeli Independence Day. The stage and balcony were a sea of blue and white, the standard uniform to match the colors of the Israeli flag. In keeping with the latest technology, the faces of the children were projected onto a large screen in the center of the room. And then it happened—what always happens when I hear children singing. I started to cry. In part my tears are connected to their innocence, the hope they represent, and their unknown future in an increasingly difficult world. Here were hundreds of children singing of their love of Israel, of the rebuilding of Zion, of the beauty of the Sabbath, of their yearning for peace and the brotherhood of man. Their voices were strong, and their faces beautiful and proud. I cried because my children were singing the same songs that I had sung and my parents and grandparents before them. I cried for the beauty of the message of the songs and for the hopes of the Jewish people expressed in these childlike voices. And the tears were also from that wellspring of emotions and memories that make up the Jewish soul.

LIFE

I call heaven and earth to witness . . . that I have set before thee
life and death, the blessing and the curse; therefore choose life,
that thou mayest live, thou and thy seed.

DEUTERONOMY 30:19

*L*IFE IS A DAUNTING SUBJECT. From Ecclesiastes to Sartre, from
the ancient sages to our modern philosophers, our greatest thinkers have been preoccupied with the nature and purpose of life.
To prepare, I turned immediately to the esteemed works of Milton Berle, Sam Levenson, and Nathan Ausubel's immense *Treasury of Jewish Humor*. What better way to distract myself and
tackle so difficult a subject? Laughter is an outlet and offers
perspective. It contains a fundamental capacity to enlarge and
relax our take on life. There is too much we do not understand,
too much tragedy, despair, and inequality. Armed with humor
and humility we can confront the serious world around us and
try to find enduring meaning in life.

Often at night, when I sit at my children's bedsides, our talk
turns to their fears. Life can feel perilous at any age. At nine,
the worries range from grades, to best friends, right on through
to intruders and illness to nothing less than death itself. I reassure
them as best I can, comfort them with the very advice I give

myself: Fears are normal, but don't let them stop you . . . think about the good things . . . take one day at a time . . . you can do it . . . believe in yourself, in others, and mostly in life . . . there's so much good out there . . .

In Judaism, a meaningful life requires one, as the prophet Micah wrote, "to do justice, love goodness, and walk modestly with your God." It requires a commitment to family and community. And our tradition teaches us that we should enjoy all the good things in life. In Deuteronomy we are told "Go eat your bread in joy and drink your wine with good cheer." Our sages teach us "In the time to come, everyone will have to account for all the things God created and we refused to enjoy."

"L'chaim," to life, is the traditional Jewish toast for all occasions. It encompasses all our wishes — for a long life, a healthy life, a life with "nachas" — that intangible satisfaction we derive from our accomplishments and those of our loved ones. In essence, everything in this book is about life itself. We define ourselves by our families, friendships, and faith. We gain continuity and spiritual vitality from the Sabbath and holidays and the beauty of the natural world; courage and inspiration from our love of Israel. We are a people of shared memories, fortified by tradition and humor. We must take the advice we give our children.

The world is a narrow bridge. The key to the crossing is not to be afraid.

NACHMAN OF BRATSLAV

There is no need for you to leave the house. Stay at your table and listen. Don't even listen, just wait. Don't even wait, be completely quiet and alone. The world will offer itself to you to be unmasked; it can't do otherwise; in raptures it will writhe before you.
FRANZ KAFKA, *Parables and Paradoxes*

Remember that life is a celebration or can be a celebration. One of the most important things is to teach man how to celebrate.
ABRAHAM HESCHEL, *Who Is Man?*

The world is new to us every morning—this is God's gift; and every man should believe he is reborn each day.
BAAL SHEM TOV

Every person born into this world represents something new, something that never existed before, something original and unique. It is the duty of every person in Israel to know and consider that he is unique in the world in his particular character and that there has never been anyone like him in the world, for if there had been someone like him, there would have been no need for him to be in the world. Every single man is a new thing in the world and is called upon to fulfill his particularity in the world.
MARTIN BUBER, *The Way of Man*

A season is set for everything, a time for every experience under heaven.
A time for being born, and a time for dying,
A time for planting and a time for uprooting the planted;
A time for slaying and a time for healing,
A time for tearing down and a time for building up;
A time for weeping and a time for laughing,
A time for wailing and a time for dancing;

A time for throwing stones and a time for gathering
   stones,
A time for embracing and a time for shunning embraces;
A time for seeking and a time for losing,
A time for keeping and a time for discarding;
A time for ripping and a time for sewing,
A time for silence and a time for speaking;
A time for loving and a time for hating;
A time for war and a time for peace.
ECCLESIASTES 3:1–8

Why did God create Adam alone? In order to teach us that
whoever destroys a single life is as guilty as though he had destroyed the entire world; and that whoever saves one life, earns
as much merit as though he had saved the entire world.
TALMUD: SANHEDRIN 4:5

I would say that behind all my ideas, the strongest idea of mine
which is conveyed in my thinking, even more than in my writing, is the freedom of choice. I feel that the freedom of choice
is the very essence of life. Although the gifts which God has
given us are small in the comparison to the gifts which He has
given maybe to the angels or to the stars, we have one great
gift—and this is to choose.
ISAAC BASHEVIS SINGER in *Isaac Bashevis Singer: Conversations*, ed.
Grace Farrell (hereinafter *Conversations*)

Who is he that is rich? He who is happy with his lot.
Ethics of the Fathers 4:1

A man should go on living—if only to satisfy his curiosity.
YIDDISH PROVERB

Experience is a good school, but the fees are high.
HEINRICH HEINE

Hope for the best. Expect the worst. Life is a play. We're unrehearsed.
MEL BROOKS, *The Twelve Chairs*

If you're going to do something wrong, at least enjoy it.
FOLK SAYING

For a long happy life, breathe through your nose and keep your mouth shut.
YIDDISH FOLK SAYING

You must learn from the mistakes of others. You can't possibly live long enough to make them all yourself.
SAM LEVENSON, *You Don't Have to Be in Who's Who to Know What's What*

Man's obsession to add to his wealth and honor is the chief source of his misery.
MAIMONIDES, *Guide of the Perplexed* 3:39

A man is, alas, only a man—and sometimes not even that.
FOLK SAYING

In a similar vein, Marshall Brickman used to say—"You only live once—if that."

Which is the right course which a man should choose for himself? That which he feels to be honorable to himself and which also brings him honor from mankind.
Ethics of the Fathers 2:1

The divine test of a man's worth is not his theology but his life.
MORRIS JOSEPH, *Judaism as Creed and Life*

A rich world lies before us, wide vistas, great depths, infinite boundless, unquestionable light. Plunge, O Man, into the depths of your heart to these currents of light and of life. Live! Live in every atom of your being! Live and you will see that there is still room for love, for faith, for idealism, for creation; and perhaps, who knows, there may yet be worlds still undreamed of.
A. D. GORDON, "Fundamentals"

A king was told that a man of humility is endowed with long life. He attired himself in old garments, took up his residence in a small hut, and forbade anyone to show reverence before him. But when he honestly examined himself, the king found himself to be prouder of his seeming humility than ever before. A Philosopher thereupon remarked to him: "Dress like a king; live like a king; allow the people to show due respect to you; but be humble in your inmost heart."
BAAL SHEM TOV

Time is life. Use it or lose it. Seize it as if you have every right to it, like air; take it in, hold it, expand it, shape it to your dreams or it will gallop out of control and disappear.
LETTY COTTIN POGREBIN, *Getting Over Getting Older*

When the individual values the community as his own life and strives after its happiness as though it were his individual well-being, he finds satisfaction and no longer feels so keenly the bitterness of his individual existence, because he sees the end for which he lives and suffers.
ACHAD HA'AM in *A Modern Treasury of Jewish Thoughts*

There is no question that there is joy in life, because if there would be no joy there wouldn't even be suffering. We wouldn't even know that we suffer because that would be the natural thing. There is joy in every life and hope in every life. And there is great joy in love and in sex and in food and seeing nature and the greatest joy is free choice.

ISAAC BASHEVIS SINGER, *Conversations*

I never think of the future; it comes soon enough.

ALBERT EINSTEIN interview, December 1930

I AM SITTING HERE

Yehudah Amichai

I am sitting here now with my father's eyes,
and with my mother's graying hair on my head,
in a house that belonged to an Arab
who bought it from an Englishman
who took it from a German
who hewed it from the stones
of Jerusalem, my city.
I look upon God's world of others
who received it from others.
I am composed of many things.
I have been collected many times.
I am constructed of spare parts
of decomposing materials
of disintegrating words. And already
in the middle of my life, I begin,
gradually, to return to them,
for I wish to be a decent and orderly person
when I'm asked at the border, "Have you anything to
    declare?"

So that there won't be too much pressure at the end,
so that I won't arrive sweating and breathless and
    confused,
so that I shan't have anything left to declare.
The red stars are my heart, the Milky Way
its blood, my blood. The hot khamsin
breathes in huge lungs, my life
pulses close to a huge heart, always within.

The central problem in the Bible is not God, but man. The Bible is a book about man, rather than man's book about God. And the great problem is how to answer, to respond to the human situation.

ABRAHAM HESCHEL, *God in Search of Man*

The Bible says, "As he came out of his mother's womb, so must he depart at last, naked as he came." (Ecclesiastes 5:14)

This might be compared to a fox who found a vineyard that was closed on all sides, except for one small hole in it.

He tried to enter, but could not.

What did he do?

He fasted for three days until he became thin and scrawny. Then he entered through the hole. He ate from the vineyard and became sleek and fat.

When he wanted to leave, he could not get through the hole. So he fasted another three days until he became thin and scrawny again.

Then he went out.

On leaving, he turned and looked at the place, saying,

"O vineyard, vineyard, how beautiful you are, and how good is your fruit. All your produce is wonderful and worthy of praise.

But what enjoyment have you given me? In the state in which one enters you, one must leave."

And so it is with the world at large.

ECCLESIASTES RABBAH 5:14

For there is no man who does not have his hour.

Ethics of the Fathers 4:3

All beginnings are difficult.

MECHILTA ON EXODUS 19:5

We are sinful not simply because we have eaten from the Tree of Knowledge, but also because we haven't eaten yet from the Tree of Life.

FRANZ KAFKA, *Parables and Paradoxes*

We do not succeed in changing things according to our desire, but gradually our desire changes. The situation that we hoped to change because it was unacceptable becomes unimportant. We have not managed to surmount the obstacle, as we were totally determined to do, but life has taken us around it, led us beyond it.

MARCEL PROUST, *Remembrance of Things Past*

Anyone who cannot cope with life while he is alive needs one hand to ward off a little of his despair over his fate . . . but with his other hand he can jot down what he sees among the ruins, for he sees different and more things than the others; after all, he is dead in his own lifetime and the real survivor.

FRANZ KAFKA, *Parables and Paradoxes*

There are only two ways to live your life. One is as though nothing is a miracle. The other is as though everything is a miracle.

ALBERT EINSTEIN

Sometimes small things lead to great joys.

S. J. AGNON

Go, eat your bread in gladness, and drink your wine in joy; for your action was long ago approved by God.

Let your clothes be always freshly washed, and your head never lack ointment.

Enjoy happiness with a woman you love, all the fleeting days of life that have been granted to you under the sun—all your fleeting days.

For that alone is what you can get out of life and out of the means you acquire under the sun.

Whatever is in your power to do, do with all your might. For there is no action, no reasoning, no learning, no wisdom in the netherworld where you are going . . .

Even if a man lives many years, let him enjoy himself in all of them, remembering how many the days of darkness are going to be. The only future is nothingness!

ECCLESIASTES 9:7–10, 11:8

The longer I lived the more I understood that there really were no lies. Whatever doesn't really happen is dreamed at night. It happens to one if it doesn't happen to another, tomorrow if not today, or a century hence if not next year. What difference can it make?

ISAAC BASHEVIS SINGER, "Gimpel the Fool"

In January 1990 the rabbi came to shul as usual to greet the older men who were his morning minyan regulars. One challenged the rabbi playfully: "Aren't you going to wish me Happy Birthday?"

"Sure, how old are you?" replied the rabbi.

"Oh, I'm forty-five today."

"Who are you kidding, you must be at least seventy-five!"

"No, today is the day I celebrate as my birthday. Forty-five years ago I was reborn when the Allies liberated me from Auschwitz. The gift of life and the gift of freedom are for me inseparable."

PRIMO LEVI in Noam Zion and David Dishon, A *Different Night*

I need suspense, not only in my novels, but in life itself. If there is not positive suspense, then there is negative suspense. A psychologist would say that this means I am in love with my grandmother, or some such. I did love her, but that's not the explanation. We need suspense in life almost as much as we need bread . . . I create suspense in my work, and fate creates it in my life.

ISAAC BASHEVIS SINGER, *Conversations*

An homage to Camp Massad. This song ("Tzachaki" in Hebrew) was sung on Saturday nights at the end of the Sabbath during the Havdalah candlelight service. The auditorium was dark except for the light from the havdalah candles burning brightly and held proudly by campers who marched down in time with this beautiful Tchernichovsky poem sung by the rest of the camp.

CREDO
Saul Tchernichovsky

Laugh, at all my dreams, my dearest;
    Laugh, and I repeat anew
That I still believe in man —
    As I still believe in you.

For my soul is not yet unsold
    To the golden calf of scorn
And I still believe in man
    And the spirit in him born.

By the passion of his spirit,
    Shall his ancient bonds be shed.
Let the soul be given freedom,
    Let the body have its bread!

Laugh, for I believe in friendship,
    And in one I still believe,
One whose heart shall beat with my heart
    And with mine rejoice and grieve.

Let the time be dark with hatred,
    I believe in years beyond,
Love at last shall bind the peoples
    In an everlasting bond.

In that day shall my own people
    Rooted in its soil arise,
Shake the yoke from off its shoulders
    And the darkness from its eyes.

Life and love and strength and action
    In their heart and blood shall beat,
And their hopes shall be both heaven
    And the earth beneath their feet.

Then a new song shall be lifted
    To the young, the free, the brave,
And the wreath to crown the singer
    Shall be gathered from my grave.

God has given us strength and spiritual powers, but we don't make complete use of them. I would say that every human being uses only a small part of . . . his potentialities.
ISAAC BASHEVIS SINGER, *Conversations*

RESUME
Dorothy Parker

Razors pain you;
Rivers are damp;
Acids stain you;
Drugs cause cramps;
Guns aren't lawful;
Nooses give;
Gas smells awful;
You might as well live.

The world is huge and there's no place to turn.
FOLK SAYING

When something does not insist on being noticed, when we aren't grabbed by the collar or struck on the skull by a presence or an event, we take for granted the very things that most deserve our gratitude.
CYNTHIA OZICK, "Riddle of the Ordinary"

As civilization advances, the sense of wonder declines. Such decline is an alarming symptom of our state of mind. Mankind will not perish for want of information; but only for want of appreciation. The beginning of our happiness lies in the understanding that life without wonder is not worth living. What we lack is not a will to believe but a will to wonder.
ABRAHAM HESCHEL, *Between God and Man*

Be master of your will, and a servant to your conscience.
HASIDIC FOLK SAYING

Getting out of bed in the morning is an act of false confidence.
JULES FEIFFER

FAITH, OR ON BEING JEWISH

*T*HERE IS NO LIE detector test to determine if we really believe
and there is no scale to measure the strength of our faith. The
Chafetz Chaim, a nineteenth-century rabbinic scholar, said, "In
the final analysis, for the believer there are no questions, for the
nonbeliever there are no answers." This has always seemed to
be a particularly poignant statement regarding faith, but in fact,
it does not allow for the questions a believer must necessarily
have or the answers that might satisfy the nonbeliever. Even a
believer must question the brutal murder of six million innocent
people as well as the senseless tragedies that occur daily in our
society. And who can experience the birth of a healthy child or
the vast expanse of the star-lit sky without, at least, sensing a
divine presence?

My heritage, my upbringing, and my education have all given
me the knowledge of faith, but the true test of faith is in the life
we lead. Judaism cares less about our theology than about our
conduct. Belief in Judaism, its rituals and values, is the springboard for an active, moral life. The strongest expression of our
faith is a life committed to good deeds, family, and community.
We invest our lives with dignity and meaning in our devotion
to those around us.

Judaism provides us with a gold standard by which we can assess our actions. Its traditions have withstood the test of time and are not altered by the passing mores of society. My grandfather, Rabbi Joseph Lookstein, of blessed memory, spoke of this in a Rosh Hashannah sermon:

> Judaism emphasizes reason, not blind faith. It stresses understanding, not intellectual surrender; knowledge and inquiry, and not helpless submission. No, for Judaism, at least, tradition is not a voice from the dead which commands "Obey me!" It is rather the thrilling call of living experience which says "Use me!"

These traditions help us to meet the challenges that we face daily. Every achievement in life is the result of some challenge, some risk, and the successful response to that challenge is nurtured by our faith and tradition.

My grandfather, a rabbi, educator, and family man, is only one of the many voices on the following pages. Although we have community standards, the individual Jewish experience is as varied and as worthy of our respect as are the mysteries in life.

"Where does God exist?" The Kotzker rebbe asked several of his followers.

"Everywhere," the surprised disciples responded.

"No," the rebbe answered. "God exists only where man lets him in."

JOSEPH TELUSHKIN, *Jewish Wisdom*

A Jew is someone who ties, who links his or her destiny to the Jewish people. Period. That is a Jew. I do not enter religious affairs.

ELIE WIESEL, "The Great Adventure"

The pursuit of knowledge for its own sake, an almost fanatical love of justice and the desire for personal independence, these are the features of the Jewish tradition which make me thank my lucky stars I belong to it.

ALBERT EINSTEIN, *The World as I See It*

No one person is alone when he can cling to a chain of tradition in which he is the latest link.

RABBI JOSEPH H. LOOKSTEIN

God, if you don't help me, I'll ask my uncle in America.

LEO ROSTEN, ed., *Treasury of Jewish Quotations*

What God does is best—probably.

FOLK SAYING

Without a love of humankind there is no love of God.

SHOLEM ASCH, *What I Believe*

From the Jewish heritage, I have derived my world outlook, a God-centered interpretation of reality in the light of which man the individual is clothed with dignity, and the career of humanity with cosmic meaning and hope; a humane morality, elevated in its aspirations yet sensibly realistic; a system of rituals which interpenetrates my daily routines and invests them with poetry and intimations of the divine.

MILTON STEINBERG, *Basic Judaism*

For man sees only what is visible, but the Lord sees into the heart.
1 SAMUEL 16:7

Believe in God through faith, and not because of miracles.
NACHMAN OF BRATSLAV

When something good happens, it's a miracle and you should wonder what God is saving up for you later.
MARSHALL BRICKMAN

Our emancipation will not be complete until we are free of the fear of being Jews.
MORDECHAI M. KAPLAN, *The Future of the American Jew*

I love every Jew except a Jew who doesn't love other Jews.
RABBI JOSEPH H. LOOKSTEIN

In the winter of 1974, while I was on retreat at the Trappist monastery in Spencer, Massachusetts, one of the monks told me, "When you know the name by which God knows you, you will know who you are."

I searched for that name with the passion of one seeking the Eternal beloved. I called myself Father, Writer, Teacher, but God did not answer.

Now I know the name by which God calls me. I am Yaakov Daniel ben Avraham v'Sarah.

I have become who I am. I am who I always was. I am no longer deceived by the black face which stares at me from the mirror.

I am a Jew.
JULIUS LESTER, *Lovesong: Becoming a Jew*

Getting inoculated with small doses of religion prevents people from catching the real thing.
SAM LEVENSON, *You Don't Have to Be in Who's Who to Know What's What*

Before we can effectively combat anti-Semitism, we must first of all educate ourselves out of it, and out of the slave-mentality which it betokens. Only when we respect ourselves, can we win the respect of others; or rather, the respect of others will then come of itself.
ALBERT EINSTEIN, *The World as I See It*

Through faith we experience the world; through action we give the world meaning.
LEO BAECK, *Essence of Judaism*

There are many advantages which Jews may derive from a knowledge and love of Judaism. It can give them a high, clear religious faith. It can supply them with a system of ethical values, personal and social, idealistic and practical at the same time. It can grace their lives with poetic observances and with the treasures of an ancient tradition. It can make them, in sum, nobler, stronger, better human beings and more valuable citizens.

But one service Judaism performs for Jews which is often overlooked: it is the first function of a human being to respect himself, to stand erect and foursquare before the world, to injure none, to help all, but to allow none to injure him—to be in sum, a man.
MILTON STEINBERG, *A Believing Jew*

To be a Jew is to be a friend of mankind, to be a proclaimer of liberty and peace.
LUDWIG LEWISOHN, *Israel*

Judaism is rooted forever in the soil, blood, life-experience and memory of a particular folk—the Jewish people.
SOLOMON GOLDMAN, *Crisis and Decision*

Being a Jew in the broadest definition means first, the accident of birth; secondly, the act of choice, choosing to remain Jewish despite the difficulties; thirdly, the act of cognition, learning to know the history and literature of his people so as to understand its soul and appreciate its place in the world; and finally, the act of transmission, transmitting to the next generation his heritage and the will to carry it on so that the Jewish people may not perish from the earth.
ISRAEL GOLDSTEIN, *Toward a Solution*

In Judaism social action is religiousness, and religiousness implies social action.
LEO BAECK, *Essence of Judaism*

The early Hebrews had created the Bible out of their lives; their descendants created their lives out of the Bible.
ABRAHAM LEON SACHAR, *A History of the Jews*

Judaism is a theology of the common deed, of the trivialities of life, dealing not so much with training for the exceptional as with management of the trivial. The predominant feature in the Jewish pattern of life is unassuming, inconspicuous piety rather than extravagance, mortification, asceticism. Thus the purpose seems to be to ennoble the common.
ABRAHAM HESCHEL, *Man Is Not Alone*

Jews are the people of the spirit, and whenever they return to the spirit, they are great and splendid and put to shame and overcome their knavish oppressors. Rosenkranz profoundly compared them to the giant Antaeus, except that the giant was

strengthened whenever he touched earth, while the Jews gain
new strength whenever they touch heaven.
HEINRICH HEINE, *Ludwig Boerne*

The rituals and disciplines that surrounded my childhood sensitized my spirit, made it permanently susceptible to the messages behind them; the names of the Patriarchs and the Kings
and holy places were permanently lodged in me, and at a later
period in my life reverberated again with those overtones which
accompany and distinguish the essential nature of tradition.
MAURICE SAMUEL, *The Professor and the Fossil*

For others, a knowledge of the history of their people is a civic
duty, while for the Jews it is a sacred duty.
MAURICE SAMUEL, *The Professor and the Fossil*

We Jews are a community based on memory. A common memory has kept us together and enabled us to survive. This does
not mean that we based our life on any one particular past, even
on the loftiest of pasts; it simply means that one generation
passed on to the next a memory which gained in scope—for
new destiny and new emotional life were constantly accruing to
it—and which realized itself in a way we can call organic. This
expanding memory was more than a spiritual motif; it was a
power which sustained, fed, and quickened Jewish existence itself.
    Much has disappeared from Jewry in the past one hundred
and fifty years, but nothing is so ominous as the disappearance
of the collective memory and the passion for handing down . . .
The passion to hand down can be replaced only by the passion
to study, the passion of the fathers only by that of the sons, who
must work unremittingly to regain the approach to the ancestral
treasure, and thus re-establish the bond of memory that joins the

community together. Whether there are many such sons or few, they constitute a beginning.

MARTIN BUBER, *Israel and the World*

Whenever I'm in trouble, I pray. And since I'm always in trouble, there is not a day when I don't pray. In many cases I get the answer even before I pray. The belief that man can do what he wants, without God, is as far as the North Pole. I don't think religion should be connected with dogma or revelation. Since he's a silent God, he talks in deeds, in events, and we have to learn this language. The belief in God is as necessary as sex. Whatever you call him — nature or higher power — doesn't matter. The power that takes care of you, and the farthest star, all this is God.

ISAAC BASHEVIS SINGER in Israel Shenker, *Coat of Many Colors*

If God were living on earth, people would probably break his windows.

YIDDISH FOLK SAYING

You feel oppressed by your Judaism only as long as you do not take pride in it.

BERTHA PAPPENHEIM

To be rooted is perhaps the most important and least recognized need of the human soul.

SIMONE WEIL

I don't believe in a monopoly. I think God loves all men. He has given many nations. He has given all men an awareness of His greatness and of His love. And God is to be found in many hearts all over the world. Not limited to one nation or to one people, to one religion.

ABRAHAM HESCHEL in an interview with Carl Stern in *Moral Grandeur*

Happy are we. How goodly is our portion, how pleasant our lot, how beautiful our heritage.
DAILY MORNING SERVICE

TO BE A JEW IN THE TWENTIETH CENTURY

Muriel Rukeyser

To be a Jew in the twentieth century
Is to be offered a gift. If you refuse,
Wishing to be invisible, you choose
Death of the spirit, the stone insanity.
Accepting, take full life. Full agonies:
Your evening deep in labyrinthine blood
Of those who resist, fail, and resist; and God
Reduced to a hostage among hostages.

The gift is torment. Not alone the still
Torture, isolation; or torture of the flesh.
That may come also. But the accepting wish,
The whole and fertile spirit as guarantee
For every human freedom, suffering to be free.
Daring to live for the impossible.

Older, sadder, wiser, I go seeking now, through faith and reason compounded, the answer to this baffling pageant which is the world, and this little by-play which has been my life.
MILTON STEINBERG, *As a Driven Leaf*

We Jews become once more conscious of our nationality, and regain the self-respect which is necessary to our national existence. We must learn once more to avow our ancestry and our history; we must once more take upon ourselves, as a nation,

cultural tasks of a kind calculated to strengthen our feeling of solidarity.
ALBERT EINSTEIN, *The World as I See It*

Religion is comparable to a childhood neurosis.
SIGMUND FREUD, *Future of an Illusion*

If you live in New York or any other big city, you are Jewish. It doesn't matter even if you're Catholic; if you live in New York, you're Jewish. If you live in Butte, Montana, you're going to be goyish even if you're Jewish . . .
    Jewish means pumpernickel bread, black cherry soda and macaroons. Goyish means Koolaid, Drake's cakes, and lime Jell-O. Trailer parks are so goyish that Jews won't go near them.
LENNY BRUCE, *How to Talk Dirty and Influence People*

Judaism is less about believing and more about belonging. It is less about what we owe God and more about what we owe each other, because we believe God cares more about how we treat each other than He does about our theology.
HAROLD S. KUSHNER, *To Life!*

Everyone should worship God in accordance with the dictates of his own conscience, and not under constraint.
JOSEPHUS, *Life*

Where there is no vision, the people perish.
PROVERBS 29:18

The center of Judaism is in the home. In contrast to other re-ligions, it is at home where the essential celebrations and acts of observance take place — rather than in the synagogue or tem-ple . . . The synagogue is an auxiliary . . . A Jewish home is where

Judaism is at home, where Jewish learning, commitment, sensitivity to values are cultivated and cherished.
ABRAHAM HESCHEL, *The Insecurity of Freedom*

You cannot command belief.
SAMUEL DAVID LUZZATTO

Miracles sometimes occur, but one has to work terribly hard for them.
CHAIM WEIZMANN

There is endless variety in the details of the customs and laws which prevail in the world at large. To give but a summary enumeration: some peoples have entrusted the supreme political power to monarchies, others to oligarchies, yet others to the masses. Our lawgiver, however, was attracted by none of these forms of polity, but gave to his constitution the form of what—if a forced expression be permitted—may be termed a "theocracy," placing all Sovereignty and authority in the hands of God.
JOSEPHUS, *Against Apion* II

Two Jews on an island will build three synagogues—one for each, and a third neither wants to attend.
LEO ROSTEN, ed., *Treasury of Jewish Quotations*

Thus said the Lord: Let not the wise man glory in his wisdom; Let not the strong man glory in his strength; Let not the rich man glory in his riches. But only in this should one glory: In his earnest devotion to Me. For I the Lord act with kindness, justice and equity in the world; For in these I delight.
JEREMIAH 9:22–23

Man doth not live by bread alone but by everything that proceedeth out of the mouth of the Lord doth man live.
DEUTERONOMY 8:3

In the communion of Judaism, the identification with my people, my active affection for the Land of Israel, my faltering efforts to live by the precepts of the Prophets, I have found a peace of the spirit. They have combined in a set of values which do not have all the answers and perhaps are yet only barely perceptible to me. It is a way of life and understanding by which, as a human being, an American, a Jew and a writer, I can view with more meaning the world around me and the world within.
MICHAEL BLANKFORT, "The Education of a Jew"

There is a plan to this universe. There is a high intelligence, maybe even a purpose, but it's given to us on the installment plan . . . I would say that man is not born to know God but to search for God. The search in itself is a way of serving God. If we search for God and we are good to human beings, we are doing more or less our job. I could never believe in this business that evolution did it all . . . Modern man is inclined to feel that there is no purpose to the universe, no sense even. There were atoms and they combined and combined, and this is how the universe came out. This to me is sheer nonsense. It is as if one would say there is a printing shop in heaven and letters were dropped down to earth and the result is Homer, de Maupassant, and the Bible. I just don't believe in this kind of nonsense.
ISAAC BASHEVIS SINGER, Conversations

"Of course I believe," said Hersh Rassayner, separating his hands in innocent wonder. "You can touch particular providence, it's so palpable. But perhaps you're thinking of the kind of man who has faith that the Almighty is to be found only in the pleasant places of this world but is not to be found, God forbid, in the

desert and wasteland? You must know the rule: Just as man must make a blessing over the good, so must he make a blessing over the evil."
CHAIM GRADE, "My Quarrel with Hersh Rassayner"

To be a Jew is to be a friend of mankind, to be a proclaimer of liberty and peace.
LUDWIG LEWISOHN, *Israel*

Faith is an act of man who, transcending himself, responds to Him who transcends the world.
ABRAHAM HESCHEL, *Between God and Man*

We are festive weepers, etching names on every stone, touched by hope, hostages of governments and history, blown by wind and gathering holy dust.
YEHUDAH AMICHAI

A religious man is a person who holds God and man in one thought at one time, at all times, who suffers harm done to others, whose greatest passion is compassion, whose greatest strength is love and defiance of despair.
ABRAHAM HESCHEL, *Man Is Not Alone*

There can be no faith without truth.
ZOHAR

CHARITY
AND LOVINGKINDNESS

It's no disgrace to be poor but it's no great honor, either.
SHOLOM ALEICHEM

*T*HE ESSENCE OF JUDAISM lies not in what we believe but in how we act. With the saintly, of course, the two are one and the same, but our sages were wise enough and practical enough to acknowledge the selfishness of human nature and insistent about our potential to overcome it. Helping someone with money or time not only benefits one who is poor or lonely, but gives meaning to the life of the person giving.

There are countless passages in the Bible that describe how we should behave toward our fellow men, particularly those who are in need. This one from Deuteronomy has always seemed especially beautiful to me: "When you reap the harvest in your field and overlook a sheaf in the field, do not turn back to get it; it shall go to the stranger, the fatherless, and the widow . . . " (Deuteronomy, 24:19–21)

In the story of Ruth, the young widow, destitute after the famine in Israel had subsided, gathers food for herself and her mother-in-law, Naomi: "And she went, and came and gleaned in the field after the reapers; and her hap was to light on the portion of the field belonging unto Boaz." (Ruth 2:3)

In Jewish tradition, the wealthy invite their poorer neighbors into their homes to partake in a meal or a celebration. Charity is not only giving money or gifts to the poor, but is lovingkindness (in Hebrew *gemilut chesed*), hospitality and time spent with another human being. My father, when approached by a poor person for money to buy food, would take the person into a coffee shop and join him in the meal. My children attend a school where charity is collected daily and community service — visiting the sick, singing for the elderly, bringing food into people's homes — is a mandate.

The obligation to help the needy and the poor is one of the most important commandments in the Bible. So much emphasis is placed on the obligation to be charitable that one Talmudic scholar, R. Assi, felt it was as important as all the other commandments combined.

Judaism does not see charity as merely a favor to the poor or as a voluntary act of grace. In fact, in a poetic vein, the rabbis imagined the world supported Atlas-like by our charitable deeds.

Naked a man comes into the world, and naked he leaves it; after all his toil, he carries away nothing — except the deeds he leaves behind.
adapted from RASHI

If there shall be a destitute person among you, any of your brethren in any of your cities . . . you shall not harden your heart or close your hand against your destitute brother. Rather, you shall open your hand to him; you shall lend him his requirement, whatever is lacking to him . . . For destitute people will not cease to exist within the Land; therefore I command you, saying, "You

shall open your hand to your brother, to your poor, and to your
destitute in your Land."
DEUTERONOMY 15:7, 11

The commandment to be charitable is in its weight as much as
all the rest of the commandments in total . . . Those who give
charity in secret are greater than Moses.
TALMUD: BAVA BATHRA 9b

Through charity and kindness a man attains to godliness.
NACHMAN OF BRATSLAV

When a person eats and drinks at the festive meal he is obligated
to provide food for the stranger, the orphan, and the widow,
along with the rest of the poor and despondent. But whoever
locks the doors of his courtyard, and eats and drinks with his
wife and children, and does not provide food and drinks for poor
or suffering people, this is not a "mitzva celebration" but a "celebration of his belly" . . . and this kind of celebration is a disgrace
for them.
MAIMONIDES, MISHNEH TORAH: LAW OF FESTIVALS 6:18

Six years shall you sow your land and gather in its produce. And
in the seventh, you shall leave it untended and unharvested, and
the destitute of your people shall eat what is left; so shall you
do to your vineyard and olive grove.
EXODUS 23:10

Lend before witnesses but give without them.
TALMUD: KETUBOTH

The greatest charity is to enable the poor to earn a living.
TALMUD: SABBATH

Whoever gives the poor money is blessed sixfold; whoever does it with a kind word is blessed sevenfold.

TALMUD: BABA BATHRA 9b

Give much or give little, only give with your heart for the sake of God.

FOLK SAYING

There are eight degrees of charity, one higher than the other. The highest degree, exceeded by none, is that of the person who assists a poor Jew by providing him with a gift or a loan or by accepting him into a business partnership or by helping him find employment — in a word, by putting him where he can dispense with other people's aid . . .

A step below this stands the person which gives alms to the needy in such a manner that the giver knows not to whom he gives and the recipient knows not from whom it is that he takes . . . An illustration would be the Hall of Secrecy in the ancient Temple, where the righteous would place their gifts clandestinely and where poor people . . . would come and secretly help themselves to succor.

The rank next to this is of him who drops money in the charity box. One should not drop money in the charity box unless one is sure that the person in charge is trustworthy, wise, and competent to handle the funds properly . . .

A step lower is that in which the poor person knows from whom he is taking but the giver knows not to whom he is giving. Examples of this were the great sages who would tie their coins in their scarves which they would fling over their shoulders so that the poor might help themselves without suffering shame.

The next degree lower is that of him who, with his own hand, bestows a gift before the poor person asks.

The next degree lower is that of him who gives less than is fitting but gives with a gracious mien.

The next degree lower is that of him who gives morosely.
MAIMONIDES, MISHNEH TORAH: LAWS CONCERNING GIFTS TO THE
POOR 10:7–14

If a person resides in a town thirty days, he becomes responsible
for contributing to the soup kitchen; three months, to the charity
box; six months, to the clothing fund; nine months, to the burial
fund; and twelve months, for contributing to the town walls.
TALMUD: BAVA BATRA 8a

Most people worry about their own financial needs and their
neighbor's soul. Better they should worry about their neighbor's
financial needs and their own souls.
RABBI ISRAEL LIPKIN SALANTER

Is this the fast I want, a day for men to starve their bodies? Is it
bending the head like a bullrush and lying in sackcloth and
ashes? Do you call that a fast, a day when the Lord is disposed
to you?

No, this is the fast I desire:

To untie the bindings of wickedness and untie the cords of
the yoke. To let the oppressed go free; to break off every yoke.

It is to share your bread with the hungry and to take the
suffering poor into your home; when you see them naked to give
them clothes, and not to ignore your own family.
ISAIAH 58:5–7

There was a terrible famine sweeping the country and a certain
tzaddik [righteous man] realized it was in his capacity to help
by going to those who could give and asking for something for
those who were starving.

Knocking at the door of a man well-known for his disregard
of others, the tzaddik made his presentation of the need and
received instead of a contribution a smack in the face.

Wiping the blood from his lower lip, the tzaddik said to the wealthy man, "The punishment was obviously for me, but now what will you give to the poor?"
HASIDIC FOLKTALE

Even a poor man who lives off charity should perform acts of charity.
BABYLONIAN TALMUD: GITTIN 7a

Before prayer, give to charity.
NACHMAN OF BRATSLAV

Happy is he that considereth the poor.
PSALM 41:2

We learn about the importance of hospitality for the first time with Abraham — the perfect host. According to the Bible, he was sitting in his tent and spied three men approaching and "he ran to meet them from the door of the tent and fetched a little water, offered them food and drink." (Genesis 18:2–6)

Hospitality to wayfarers is greater than welcoming the presence of the Shechinah [God].
TALMUD: SHABBAT 127a

He who has fed a stranger may have fed an angel.
TALMUD

Give of yourself . . . you can always give something, even if it is only kindness . . . no one has ever become poor from giving.
ANNE FRANK, *The Diary of a Young Girl*, March 1944

The purpose of the laws of the Torah . . . is to bring mercy, loving kindness and peace upon the world.

MAIMONIDES, MISHNEH TORAH: LAWS OF THE SABBATH 2:3

Where [our sages asked] shall we look for the Messiah? Shall the Messiah come to us on clouds of glory, robed in majesty, and crowned with light? The [Babylonian] Talmud (Sanhedrin 98a) reports that Rabbi Joshua ben Levi put this question to no less an authority than the prophet Elijah himself.

"Where," Rabbi Joshua asked, "shall I find the Messiah?"

"At the gate of the city," Elijah replied.

"How shall I recognize him?"

"He sits among the lepers."

"Among the lepers?" cried Rabbi Joshua. "What is he doing there?"

"He changes their bandages," Elijah answered. "He changes them one by one."

That may not seem like much for a Messiah to be doing. But, apparently, in the eyes of God, it is a mighty thing indeed.

RABBI ROBERT KIRSCHNER, Sermon on AIDS in Albert Vorspan and David Saperstein, *Tough Choices*

Troubles no one wants to steal from you; good deeds no one can.

FOLK SAYING

The beginning and the end [of Torah] is the performance of lovingkindness.

TALMUD: SOTAH 14a

The whole value of a benevolent deed lies in the love that inspires it.

TALMUD: SUKKAH 49b

Once, when Abbah Tahnah the Pious was entering his city on Sabbath eve at dusk, a bundle slung over his shoulder, he came upon a man afflicted with boils lying helplessly at a crossroads.

The man said to him, "Master, do an act of kindness for me. Carry me into the city."

Abbah Tahnah replied, "If I abandon my bundle, how shall I and my household support ourselves? But if I abandon a man afflicted with boils, I will forfeit my life!"

What did he do? He let his good inclination overpower his evil inclination [set down his bundle on the road], and carried the afflicted man into the city. Then he returned for his bundle and reentered the city with the last rays of the sun. Everybody was astonished [at seeing so pious a man carrying his bundle when the Sabbath was about to begin, and during which it is forbidden to carry], and exclaimed, "Is this really Abbah Tahnah the Pious?"

He too felt uneasy at heart and said to himself: "Is it possible that I have desecrated the Sabbath?"

At that point the Holy One caused the sun to continue to shine [thereby delaying the Sabbath's beginning].

Ecclesiastes Rabbah 9:7

Happy is the man whose deeds are greater than his learning.

Midrash: Eliyahu Rabbah 17

The man whose good deeds exceed his wisdom is like a tree with few branches and many roots: all the raging winds will not move him.

Ethics of the Fathers 3:17

God looks at a man's heart before He looks at a man's brains.

FOLK SAYING

The heart can ennoble any calling: A kind jailer may exceed the saintly in true merit, and a jester may be first in the kingdom of heaven, if they have diminished the sadness of human lives.
TALMUD

There is an old saying: If you wish to find out whether your motive is pure, test yourself in two ways: whether you expect recompense from God or anyone else, and whether you would perform the act in the same way if you were alone, unbeknown to others.
BACHYA IBN PAKUDA, *Duties of the Heart*

When I was young, I admired clever people. Now that I am old, I admire kind people.
ABRAHAM HESCHEL

A rich man once came to the maggid of Koznitz.
"What are you in the habit of eating?" the maggid asked.
"I am modest in my demands," the rich man replied. "Bread and salt, and a drink of water are all I need."
"What are you thinking of!" the rabbi reproved him. "You must eat roast meat and drink mead, like all rich people." And he did not let the man go until he had promised to do as he said. Later the Hasidim asked him the reason for this odd request.
"Not until he eats meat," said the maggid, "will he realize the poor man needs bread. As long as he himself eats bread, he will think the poor man can live on stones."
MARTIN BUBER, *Tales of the Hasidim*

A newly created concrete reality has been laid in our arms; we answer for it. A dog has looked at you, you answer for its glance,

a child has clutched your hand, you answer for its touch, a host of men move about you, you answer for their need.
MARTIN BUBER, *Between Man and Man*

Say little and do much.
Ethics of the Fathers 1:15

ETHICS

*T*HE MOST PROFOUND AFFIRMATION of the dignity of man is found in the first chapter of Genesis where we are told that God created Adam and Eve in His image. Any malevolence toward God's creations is an affront to Him in whose image we are all created. This is the foundation of all Jewish ethics, the daunting mandate to do as He would do.

In Leviticus 19:18 that charge achieves its most noble expression in the universally comprehensive maxim of morality—the golden rule of human conduct: "Thou shalt not take vengeance nor bear any grudge against the children of thy people but thou shalt love thy neighbor as thyself, I am the Lord."

The story is told of a heathen who came to Shammai. Shammai and Hillel were the leading rabbis of the period at the end of the second temple in Jerusalem. The Talmud relates that the heathen said to Shammai, "Convert me to Judaism on condition that you teach me the whole Torah while I stand on one foot." Shammai, enraged by his arrogant behavior, chased him away. When he came before Hillel, Hillel converted him and said, "What is hateful to you, do not do to your neighbor. This is the whole of Torah. The rest is commentary; now go study."

And to this day, we are still studying. Some of the biblical and talmudic proscriptions are startlingly precise. There are rulings on business practices that include scrupulous evaluation of everything from scales and measures to the rights and consideration of laborers.

From each ancient edict, we can extract the principles that still apply. But the true measure of an ethical life is less easily delineated, those balances and weights of our own conscience are uneven and exposed to distractions and gratifications unimagined by our sages. These are not easy times for those who seek to live by scruples. From reading the paper or watching the evening news, one can feel as if no ethical consensus exists. I am often surprised by the person who practices many religious rituals but is corrupt in his work or behaves immorally in his family. Within each of us, no doubt, lies the power for more decency in our homes, in our work, and in our world.

When a man appears before the Throne of Judgment, the first question he will be asked is not "Have you believed in God?" or "Have you prayed and observed the ritual?"—but "Have you dealt honorably with your fellow man?"

TALMUD: SHABBAT 31a

From both the philosophic and pedagogic points of view, one ought to come to morality before one comes to holiness. Or, to put it another way; one cannot be a tzaddik without being a mensch first.

RABBI HASKEL LOOKSTEIN, Rosh Hashannah sermon, 1980

You shall not render an unfair decision: do not favor the poor nor show deference to the rich; judge your kinsman fairly.

LEVITICUS 19:15

Distance yourself from a false word . . . do not accept a bribe, for the bribe will blind those who see and corrupt words that are just.

EXODUS 23:7–8

You shall not abuse a needy and destitute laborer, whether a fellow countryman or a non-citizen in your communities. You must pay him his wages on the same day, before the sun sets, for he is needy and urgently depends on it; else he will cry to the Lord against you, and you will incur guilt.

DEUTERONOMY 24:14–15

Whoever withholds an employee's wages, it is as though he has taken the person's life from him.

TALMUD: BAVA MEZIA

If a person hires workmen and asks them to work in the early morning or late evening, at a place where it is not the local custom to work early or late at night, he cannot force them to do so. Where it is customary to provide food for workmen, he must do so. If it is customary to give them dessert, he must do so — it all depends on local custom.

MISHNA: BAVA MEZIA 7:1

There are laws pertaining to the employees as well.

Just as the employer is enjoined not to deprive the poor worker of his wages or withhold it from him when it is due, so is the worker enjoined not to deprive the employer of the benefit of his work by idling away his time, a little here and a little there, thus wasting the whole day deceitfully . . . Indeed, the worker must be very punctual in the matter of time.

MAIMONIDES, MISHNEH TORAH: LAWS CONCERNING HIRING 13:7

When a man gives an account of what befell him at the fair, he must always be considerate of the feelings of his neighbors . . . So, for instance, if I went out to the fair—in a manner of speaking, of course, for I never attended fairs except as a child, with my father—when I went out to the fair and did well, sold everything at a good profit, and returned with pocketfuls of money, my heart bursting with joy, I never failed to tell my neighbors that I had lost every kopek and was a ruined man. Thus I was happy, and my neighbors were happy. But if, on the contrary, I had really been cleaned out at the fair, and brought home with me a bitter heart and a bellyful of green gall, I made sure to tell my neighbors that never since God made fairs had there been a better one. You get my point? For thus I was miserable and my neighbors were miserable with me.

SHOLOM ALEICHEM, *The Old Country*

You find that a man is given three names—one that his father and his mother call him, one that his fellow men call him, and one that he acquires. The one he acquires for himself is better than all the others.

MIDRASH: TANHUMA, VA-YAK'HEL

Responsibility is the navel-string of creation.

MARTIN BUBER, *Between Man and Man*

Above all, my children, be honest in money matters with Jews and non-Jews alike. If you have money or possessions belonging to other people, take better care of them than you would if they were your own. The first question that is put to a man on entering the next world is whether or not he was faithful in his business dealing. A man may work ever so hard to amass money dishonestly; he may, during his lifetime, provide his children with rich dowries and leave them a generous inheritance at his death; and yet, I say, woe shall it be to that wicked man who, because he tried to enrich his children with dishonest money, has forfeited his share in the world to come! In one fleeting moment he has lost eternity!

GLUCKEL OF HAMELN, *The Memoirs of Gluckel of Hameln*

A Proper Answer

They asked a Jew of Chelm, "What would you do if you found a million rubles in the market place and knew who had lost them? Would you withstand the temptation and return the money?"

The Jew of Chelm answered, quick as a flash, "If I knew that the money was Rothschild's I'm afraid I couldn't withstand the temptation and would not return it. But if I knew that the million rubles belonged to the poor *shammes* of the old synagogue I'd return it to the last penny."

from *A Treasury of Yiddish Stories*, ed. Irving Howe and Eliezer Greenberg

Love truth and uprightness—the ornaments of the soul—and cleave unto them; prosperity so obtained is built on a sure rock. Keep firmly to thy word; let not a legal contract or witnesses be more binding than thy verbal promise, whether in public or in private. Disdain reservations and subterfuges, evasions and sharp practices. Woe to him who builds his house upon them. . . .

MAIMONIDES

The following biblical and Talmudic passages sound almost like a spoof both in the language and attention to detail, but they are the real thing. They demonstrate how concerned the sages were with honesty and fairness in business. One wishes that the amount

of time and analysis covered in the Mishna and subsequent arguments in the Talmud could have a little more bearing on business practices today.

You shall not falsify measures of length, weight, or capacity. You shall have an honest balance, honest weights, an honest *ephah*, and an honest *hin* [kinds of measures].

LEVITICUS 19:35–36

You shall not have in your pouch alternate weights, larger and smaller. You shall not have in your house alternate measures, a larger and a smaller.

You must have completely honest weights and completely honest measures if you are to endure long on the soil that the Lord your God is giving you.

For everyone who does those things, everyone who deals dishonestly, is abhorrent to the Lord your God.

DEUTERONOMY 25:13–16

Rabbi Judah said: A shopkeeper must not give roasted corn and nuts to children [sent by their mothers to shop] because this encourages them to come only to him [creating unfair competition].

But the sages permit it.

Nor may a shopkeeper sell below the market price.

But the sages say, if he does, he is to be remembered for good!

MISHNA: BAVA MEZIA 4:12

A wholesaler must clean his measures every thirty days and a small producer, once in twelve months. Rabban Simeon ben Gamliel says the reverse is true [a small producer should clean his weights more often because without constant use they may become sticky and unbalanced].

In addition, a shopkeeper must clean his measures twice a

week, polish his weights once a week, and clean off his scales after every weighing.

MISHNA: BAVA BATRA 5:10

There is an unmistakable distinction between fraudulent and honest persuasion. It is perfectly proper to point out to the buyer any good quality which the thing for sale really possesses. Fraud consists of hiding the defects in one's wares . . .

MOSES LUZZATTO, *The Path of the Upright*

Chelm Justice

A great calamity befell Chelm one day. The town cobbler murdered one of his customers. So he was brought before the judge who sentenced him to die by hanging.

When the verdict was read a townsman arose and cried out, "If your Honor pleases — you have sentenced to death the town cobbler! He's the only one we've got. If you hang him who will mend our shoes?"

"Who? Who?" cried all the people of Chelm with one voice.

The judge nodded in agreement and reconsidered his verdict.

"Good people of Chelm," he said, "what you say is true. Since we have only one cobbler it would be a great wrong against the community to let him die. As there are two roofers in the town let one of them be hanged instead!"

from A *Treasury of Jewish Folklore*, ed. Nathan Ausubel

The Merchant from Brisk

A merchant from Brisk ordered a consignment of dry-goods from Lodz. A week later he received the following letter: "We regret we cannot fill this order until full payment has been made on the last one."

The merchant sent his reply: "Please cancel the new order. I cannot wait that long."

from A *Treasury of Jewish Folklore*, ed. Nathan Ausubel

A person who walks his path in life without regard to ethical standards is like a blind man who does not know his journey is along the bank of a river.

The person can at any moment succumb to the dangers of a wrong step and the odds are more certainly toward his being hurt than escaping harm.

MOSES LUZZATTO, *The Path of the Upright*

You shall not steal; you shall not deal falsely, nor lie one to another . . . Thou shalt not oppress thy neighbour, nor rob him; the wages of a hired servant shall not abide with thee all night until the morning."

LEVITICUS 19:11, 13

The Worriers of Chelm

The people of Chelm were worriers. So they called a meeting to do something about the problem of worry. A motion was duly made and seconded to the effect that Yossel, the cobbler, be retained by the community as a whole, to do its worrying, and that his fee be one ruble per week.

The motion was about to carry, all speeches having been for the affirmative, when one sage propounded the fatal question: "If Yossel earned a ruble a week, what would he have to worry about?"

from A *Treasury of Jewish Folklore*, ed. Nathan Ausubel

Surely, human affairs would be far happier if the power in men to be silent were the same as that to speak. But experience more than sufficiently teaches that men govern nothing with more difficulty than their tongues.
BARUCH SPINOZA, *Ethics*

Be the master of your will, and the slave of your conscience.
HASIDIC FOLK SAYING

God does not predetermine whether a man shall be righteous or wicked; that He leaves to man himself.
MIDRASH: TANHUMA, PIKKUDE 3

Now, more than any time previous in human history, we must arm ourselves with an ethical code so that each of us will be aware that he is protecting the moral merchandise absent of which life is not worth living.
SHOLEM ASCH, *What I Believe*

Righteousness and justice are the foundation of Thy throne; Mercy and truth go before thee.
PSALM 89:15

Which is the right course which a man should choose for himself? That which he feels to be honorable to himself and which also brings him honor from mankind.
Ethics of the Fathers 2:1

Rabbi Safra was once saying his morning prayers when a customer came to buy his donkey. Because he refused to interrupt his prayers, Rabbi Safra did not answer. Interpreting the rabbi's silence as disapproval of the price offered, the buyer raised his price. When the rabbi still did not answer, the buyer raised his offer again.

After the rabbi finished his prayers, he said to the buyer, "I had decided to sell you my donkey at the first price you mentioned, but I did not want to interrupt my prayers to speak to you. Therefore you may have it at that price—I will not accept the higher bids."
AHA OF SHABHA, SHE'ILTOT in Francine Klagsbrun, *Voices of Wisdom*

If err we must, let us err on the side of tolerance.
FELIX FRANKFURTER in *The New York Times Magazine*, November 23, 1952

He who would distinguish the true from the false must have an adequate idea of what is true and false.
BARUCH SPINOZA, *Ethics*

All Israelites are held responsible for one another.
TALMUD: SHEVUOTH 39a

I don't need to make a decision to eat breakfast. When I say making a decision, I mean making a decision against my desires. The Ten Commandments are commandments against human nature. Many people would like to steal if they knew that they could do it without being punished. It is also their nature to commit adultery if they can have their way without too much trouble. But Moses came and he said that if humanity wants to exist it has to follow certain rules no matter how difficult they are. I would say that even to this day we have not yet convinced ourselves that people can make such decisions and keep them. Even when they make them, they can only keep them if they make them as a collective. If people live together like the Jews in the ghettos they keep to their decisions. Why? Because one guards the other. In a collective, if a Jew wanted to commit adultery, there were many in the little ghetto who would have learned about it and they would have a great outcry to stop it.

Isaac Bashevis Singer, *Conversations*

FRIENDSHIP, LOVE,
AND MARRIAGE

I HAVE ALWAYS LOVED LANGUAGE. Whether it was Hebrew and Latin through high school, French in college, or my current fling, Italian, each one continues to hold its own romance for me. Each one conveys universal thoughts in its own discrete cadences. It strikes me that friendship too is a language, with an idiom of its own, the shorthand of shared experiences and common ground.

For the last twenty years, my husband has spent one week of his precious vacation time skiing or camping with three friends he has had since childhood — four utterly dissimilar men bound together by their earliest memories, their shared values, and their commitment to remain close. Over the years of packing, Advil and antacids have joined the sunscreen and skis. It is an endearing, and I have to admit, somewhat mysterious annual event. The mystery lies in *their* language: a private foreign tongue.

The contrast between how men and women communicate isn't news. Lately it's fodder for a flood of "relationship" books. To me, the distinctions are curious but not debilitating. I can usually get my message across the breach, and I count some very special men among my dearest friends. But there is a part of me that lives solely in the company of women I have known for years: trusted compatriots in the battle we all fight to stay true to ourselves. It is always time well spent in our common language — whether we chew on gossip or philosophy, recipes or the ingredients of a good marriage; whether we talk a lot or not at all. I have old friends and new friends and though the accents vary with our histories, I share with all of them the common vernacular of the female heart and mind. We have gotten one another through love affairs, family celebrations, promotions, illnesses, and loss. Without them, without their insights and mutual support, without the shorthand of friendship that conveys so much — in a word or a glance — I would not be completely myself.

Apart from the legendary bond between Naomi and her daughter-in-law Ruth, the Bible makes no reference to female camaraderie and loyalty. Jonathan and David are often cited as the paradigm of biblical friendship: so devoted that "Jonathan's soul became bound up with the soul of David . . . [Jonathan] loved him as himself." (1 Samuel 18:1) As with every model the Bible gives us, the standards are monumental. But then, why should we be offered anything less? The ideals are meant to inspire, not to daunt us.

All four of my daughters are blessed with the talent for friendship — I have the phone bills to prove it. Children in all sizes emerge from bedrooms here on Saturday and Sunday mornings and they're not all mine. I never seem to have enough pillows or orange juice in the house; however, I know that my daughters' lives will be richer and happier for the ability to share themselves. This afternoon over pizza, someday over a quick cup of coffee, they'll warm themselves in the fluent language of friendship.

If I am not for myself, who will be for me? And if I am only for myself, what am I: And if not now, when?
Ethics of the Fathers 1:14

If anyone tells you that he loves God and does not love his fellow man, you will know that he is lying.
MARTIN BUBER, *Ten Rungs: Hasidic Sayings*

Without love of humankind, there is no love of God.
SHOLEM ASCH

Old friends like old wine don't lose their flavor.
YIDDISH FOLK SAYING

Friendship: one heart in two bodies.
IBN ZABARA, *Book of Delight*

R. Hanina ben Dosa used to say: If a man is liked by his fellow men, he is liked by God; if he is not liked by his fellow men, he is not liked by God.
Ethics of the Fathers 3:13

Do not condemn your friend: you do not know what you would have done in his place.
HILLEL

If you seek a faultless friend, you will remain friendless.
FOLK SAYING

It is easy to acquire an enemy, difficult to acquire a friend.
YALKUT VA-ETHANNAN 845

Who is the mightiest of the mighty? He who turns his enemy into his friend.
AVOT DE RABBI NATHAN 23

This is what the Holy One said to Israel: My children, what do I seek from you? I seek no more than that you love one another and honor one another.

Tanna d'Bai Eliyahu

Rabbi Moshe of Leib of Sassov told this story: "How to love men is something I learned from a peasant. He was sitting in an inn along with other peasants, drinking. For a long time he was as silent as all the rest, but when he was moved by the wine, he asked one of the men seated beside him: 'Tell me, do you love me or don't you love me?' The other replied: 'I love you very much.' But the first peasant replied: 'You say that you love me, but you do not know what I need. If you really loved me, you would know.' The other had not a word to say to this, and the peasant who had put the question fell silent again. But I understood. To know the needs of men and to bear the burden of their sorrow—that is the true love of men."

MARTIN BUBER, *Tales of the Hasidim*

Despise no man and consider nothing impossible. For there is no man who does not have his hour, and there is nothing that does not have its place.

Ethics of the Fathers 4:3

There were two close friends who had been parted by war so that they lived in different kingdoms. Once one of them came to visit his friend, and because he came from the city of the king's enemy, he was imprisoned and sentenced to be executed as a spy.

No amount of pleas would save him, so he begged the king for one kindness.

"Your Majesty," he said, "let me have just one month to return to my land and put my affairs in order so my family will be cared for after my death. At the end of the month I will return to pay the penalty."

"How can I believe you will return?" answered the king. "What security can you offer?"

"My friend will be my security," said the man. "He will pay for my life with his if I do not return."

The king called in the man's friend, and to his amazement, the friend agreed to the conditions.

On the last day of the month, the sun was setting, and the man had not yet returned. The king ordered his friend killed in his stead. As the sword was about to descend, the man returned and quickly placed the sword on his own neck. But his friend stopped him.

"Let me die for you," he pleaded.

The king was deeply moved. He ordered the sword taken away and pardoned them both.

"Since there is such great love and friendship between the two of you," he said, "I entreat you to let me join you as a third." And from that day on they became the king's companions.

And it was in this spirit that our sages of blessed memory said, "Get yourself a companion."

ADOLF JELLINEK, "Beit ha-Midrash," in Francine Klagsbrun, *Voices of Wisdom*

What you love for yourself, love also for your fellow man.
FALAQUERA, *Sefer ha-Mevakesh*

Who finds a faithful friend finds a treasure.
APOCRYPHA: BEN SIRA 6:14

Friendship among young people, friendship that is completely independent, is one of the purest elements in a man's soul, the highest sublimation of the erotic. Happy is the man who is privileged to have it in his youth, for it will be a blessing to him all the days of his life.

CHAIM NACHMAN BIALIK in Mordecai Ovadyahu, *Bialik Speaks*

Here is an infallible test. Imagine yourself in a situation where you are alone, wholly alone on earth, and you are offered one of the two, books or men. I often hear men prizing their solitude, but that is only because there are still men somewhere on earth, even though in the far distance. I knew nothing of books when I came forth from the womb of my mother, and I shall die without books, with another human hand in my own. I do indeed, close my door at times and surrender myself to a book, but only because I can open the door again and see a human being looking at me.

MARTIN BUBER, *Pointing the Way*

Take the advice of your companion, but don't abandon that of your own heart; that is, receiving advice can be beneficial, but remain faithful to your own heart.

SEPHARDIC PROVERB

I was sitting on a beach one summer day, watching two children, a boy and a girl, playing in the sand. They were hard at work building an elaborate sand castle by the water's edge, with gates and towers and moats and internal passages. Just when they had nearly finished their project, a big wave came along and knocked it down, reducing it to a heap of wet sand. I expected the children to burst into tears, devastated by what had happened to all their hard work. But they surprised me. Instead, they ran up the shore away from the water, laughing and holding hands, and sat down to build another castle. I realized that they had taught me an important lesson. All the things in our lives, all the complicated structures we spend so much time and energy creating, are built on sand. Only our relationships to other people endure.

Sooner or later, the wave will come along and knock down what we have worked so hard to build up. When that happens, only the person who has somebody's hand to hold will be able to laugh.
HAROLD KUSHNER, *When All You've Ever Wanted Isn't Enough*

When you care about a person . . . you accept this person is in your life, and for me that's it . . . This person is a permanent part of me.
LYNNE SHARON SCHWARTZ in Letty Cottin Pogrebin, *Getting Over Getting Older*

I've loved you like a friend, the way thousands of women feel about other women.
LILLIAN HELLMAN, *The Children's Hour*

If you see love as a compromise, a defeat, you're mistaken. It's a victory. Above all in time of war, when men are filled with death, this is the time to love. This is the time to choose. An act of love may tip the balance.
ELIE WIESEL, *Gates of the Forest*

Bring all men into friendship with you.
APOCRYPHA: ARISTEAS 228

The Jewish religion has always been sensitive to the need of sentiment in our lives and to its role as a most enriching source of inspiration. Expressions of tenderness, Judaism has taught us, add poetry to our lives . . . They drive out dullness and monotony, and introduce color and meaning. Life without sentiment is like a world without flowers and without music.
RABBI BARUCH SILVERSTEIN, *A Jew in Love*

Existence is of little interest save on days when the dust of re-
alities is mingled with magic sand, when some trivial incident
becomes a springboard for romance.
MARCEL PROUST, *Within a Budding Grove*

When we are in love, our love is too big a thing for us to be
able altogether to contain within ourselves. It radiates toward the
loved one, finds there a surface . . . forcing it to return . . . and it
is this repercussion of our own feeling which we call the other's
feelings . . .
MARCEL PROUST, *Swann's Way*

Three things can't be hidden: coughing, poverty, and love.
FOLK SAYING

There is nothing like desire for preventing the things one says
from bearing any resemblance to what one has in one's mind.
MARCEL PROUST, *Guermantes Way*

Love is not the dying moan of a distant violin—it's the triumphant twang of a bedspring.
S. J. PERELMAN

Love is everything that enhances, widens, and enriches our life.
FRANZ KAFKA, *Letters to Felice*

The emotions and man are the same. And I'm interested, especially, in the emotions that become passions . . . There is nothing that cannot become a passion. Especially if they are
connected either with sex or the supernatural—and I would say
for me sex and the supernatural go very much together. I feel
that the desire of one human being for another is not only a
desire of the body but also of the soul.
ISAAC BASHEVIS SINGER, *Conversations*

There are three views of life that . . . are considered beautiful in the eyes of the Lord and of man: harmony between brothers, closeness among neighbors, and a man and his wife who are as one.

Wisdom of Ben Sira

. . . love is difficult. In a special sense it is difficult to attain. Find and give what you can in love. The future of a human being is less if love means just sleeping around. Love is something more. It comes back to the definition of life. What is life — these 60 to 70 years we have? What can we do with it if we do not love?

BERNARD MALAMUD, *Conversations with Bernard Malamud*, ed., Lawrence Lasher

Two are better than one; because they have a good reward for their labor. For if they fall, the one will lift up his fellow; but woe to him that is alone when he falleth, and hath not another to lift him up. Again, if two lie together, they have warmth; but how can one be warm alone?

ECCLESIASTES 4:9–12

Existence will remain meaningless for you if you yourself do not penetrate into it with active love and if you do not in this way discover its meaning for yourself. Everything is waiting to be hallowed by you; it is waiting for this meaning to be disclosed and to be realized by you . . . Meet the world with the fullness of your being and you shall meet God. If you wish to believe, love!

MARTIN BUBER, *At the Turning*

Marriage has to follow friendship and love because when we are really lucky, we fall in love with someone, we marry and then that person becomes our best friend. The order may vary from relationship to relationship but friendship and love are the necessary in-

gredients. And like all friendships, tolerance and compromise are essential. There are always conflicts and grievances, from the simple "why can't he put the toilet paper on the toilet paper holder?" to much more serious issues of child rearing, religious practices, political and cultural tastes—but the key is a strong basis of friendship and love, although it's not always easy . . .

A Roman noblewoman asked R. Yose ben Halafta, "In how many days did the Holy One create His world?" R. Yose replied, "In six days." She asked, "And what has He been doing since?" R. Yose replied, "The Holy One has been busy making matches: the daughter of So-and-so to So-and-so." The noblewoman said, "If that is all He does, I can do the same thing. How many menservants, how many maidservants do I have! In no time at all, I can match them up." R. Yose: "Matchmaking may be a trivial thing in your eyes; but for the Holy One, it is as awesome an act as splitting the Red Sea."

R. Yose ben Halafta left the noblewoman and went away. What did she do? She took a thousand menservants and a thousand maidservants, lined them up in row upon row facing one another, and said, "This man shall marry that woman, and this woman shall be married to that man," and so she matched them all up in a single night. In the morning, the ones thus matched came to the lady, one with his head bloodied, one with her eye knocked out, one with his shoulder dislocated, and another with her leg broken. She asked, "What happened to you?" One replied, "I don't want that woman," and another replied, "I don't want that man."

The noblewoman promptly sent to have R. Yose ben Halafta brought to her. She said to him, "Master, your Torah is completely right, excellent, and worthy of praise. All you said is exactly so."

Genesis Rabbah 68:4

The Lord God said, "It is not good for man to be alone; I will make a fitting helper for him . . . Therefore shall a man leave his father and his mother, and shall cleave unto his wife; and they shall be one flesh."
GENESIS 2:18, 24

There was a tradition in ancient Israel that when a boy was born, a cedar tree was planted and when a girl was born, a pine tree. When they grew up and married, the wedding canopy was made of branches taken from both trees.
TALMUD: GITTEN 57a

When a soul comes down from Heaven, it is both male and female. The male aspects enter a male child and the female aspects enter a female child. If they are deserving, God will cause them to find each other and to join in marriage. This is a true union.
ZOHAR

A father is forbidden to marry off his daughter while she is a minor. He must wait until she is a grown up and says, "I want so-and-so."
TALMUD: KIDDUSHIN 41a

> I am a rose of Sharon,
> A lily of the valleys.
> As a lily among thorns,
> So is my love among the daughters.
> As an apple-tree among the trees of the wood,
> So is my beloved among the sons.
> Under its shadow I delighted to sit,
> And its fruit was sweet to my taste.
> SONG OF SONGS 2:1–3

A man had two wives, a young one and an old one. The young wife pulled out his white hair, and the old one pulled out his black hair. In the end, the poor man was left with no hair at all.
TALMUD: BAVA KAMMA 60b

When our love was strong, we could lie on the edge of a sword. Now that our love is not, a bed of sixty cubits wide is not wide enough for us.
TALMUD: SANHEDRIN 7a

Love at first sight is easy to understand. It's when two people have been looking at each other for years that it becomes a miracle.
SAM LEVENSON, *You Don't Have to Be in Who's Who to Know What's What*

The story is told of a woman in Sidon who lived ten years with her husband without bearing a child. Deciding to part from each other, the two came to R. Simeon ben Yohai, who asked them, "By your lives, even as you were paired over food and drink, so must you be parted over food and drink." They followed his advice and, declaring the day a festal day for themselves, prepared a great feast, during which the wife gave her husband too much to drink. In his resulting good humor, he said to her, "My dear, pick any desirable article you want in my home, and take it with you when you return to your father's house." What did she do? After he fell asleep, she beckoned to her menservants and maidservants, and said to them, "Pick him up, couch and all, and carry him to my father's house." At midnight, he woke up from his sleep. The effects of the wine had left him, and he asked her, "My dear, where am I?" She replied, "You are in my father's house." He: "But what am I doing in your father's house?" She: "Did you not say to me last night, 'Pick any desirable article you want in my home and take it with you when you return to your father's house'? There is no desirable article in the world I care for more than for you." So they again went to R. Simeon ben Yohai, and he stood up and prayed for them, and they were remembered [by God and granted children].

Song of Songs Rabbah 1:4

Dear Katie and Arthur,

Your announcement that your daughter Jane is marrying an obscure quack named Heimlich on June 3rd saddened me considerably. I've had my eye on Jane for a long time and always hoped that some day you would wind up as my in-laws. Well, she made her choice—one that, I believe, she will ultimately regret. With me, each day would have been 24 hours of gaiety and laughter; with Heimlich she will have a life of viruses, vaccines, surgical instruments and rubber gloves. Only time can decide whether she made the right decision.

Even though I am a bitter, disappointed and disillusioned man I send them both my heartiest congratulations.

Best,
Groucho

P.S. Note to Jane: See that all his nurses are ugly.

Groucho Marx, *The Groucho Letters*

I am continually fascinated by the sages' attention to certain details. In the following excerpt, one learns that sexual responsibilities were based on the husband's profession:

For men of independent means, every day. For laborers, twice weekly. For donkey drivers [who travel about during the week], once a week; for camel-drivers [who travel for long periods], once every thirty days; for sailors [who may travel for months], once every six months.

Mishna: Ketubot 5:5

A woman prefers little food and sexual indulgence to much food
and continence.
MISHNA: SOTAH 3:4

A Jewish daughter should not be forced to marry.
YIDDISH SAYING

Love is beautiful accompanied by a tasty meal.
YIDDISH SAYING

It is said that in some parts of Africa a man doesn't know who
his wife is until he marries her. This is also true in Europe, and
in Asia, and in America, and in Brooklyn . . .
SAM LEVENSON, *You Don't Have to Be in Who's Who to Know What's
What*

> Great care a man must take
>   To show due honor to his spouse!
> Since only for his wife's sweet sake
>   Do blessings rest upon his house.
> TALMUD: BAVA METZIA 59a

THE GOLDEN PEACOCK
Chaim Nachman Bialik

> The golden peacock flies away.
> Where are you flying, pretty bird?
> I fly across the sea.
> Please ask my love to write a word,
> To write a word to me!
> I know your love, and I shall bring
> A letter back, to say,
> With a thousand kisses, that for spring
> He plans the wedding day.

One hour after Noam's proposal and my immediate and euphoric acceptance, I was standing out on the golf course in front of the Graduate College searching the darkened skies for three stars. Let me explain.

The minute Noam proposed to me I wanted to tell my mother. That was about the second or third thought that flashed through my triumphant head . . . Not that my mother and I are that close. Quite the contrary. But I very much wanted to tell someone the news, someone who would consider it momentous. And my mother, who had greeted each announcement of my educational plans with "Nu, Renee, is this going to help you find a husband?" so that the consequence of all my academic honors . . . was only a deepening sense of failure; my mother, who had always taught me that a woman is who she marries, that "there's more than one hole a man has to fill in a woman": my mother was such a person. Noam had proposed to me on a Saturday evening. My mother would not answer the phone until three stars were visible, indicating that the skies had truly darkened and Shabbos was over. That night in June, Shabbos wasn't over until after nine.

"*Gute voch,*" she answered the phone. (The Yiddish phrase means "good week.")

"Hi, Mom, it's me."

"Renee! *Gevalt!* Is something wrong? What's the matter?"

"No, Mom, what makes you say that?"

"Well, here you are calling a minute after *Havdalah,* so anxious." (*Havdalah* is a ceremony that uses wine, a candle, and sweet-smelling spices to bid farewell to the Sabbath . . .) "Of course, maybe you didn't know it was a minute after *Havdalah.* Maybe you didn't even know that today was Shabbos?"

"Sure, Mom, I knew. I just came in from counting the stars."

"Renee darling, you're keeping Shabbos?"

"No, Mom, I just knew it would be futile to try and call you too early."

"Nu, so at least you still remember a little something. If you still remember, there's hope."

"Listen, Mom, I have something to tell you."

"I'm listening."

"I'm getting married."

A gasp. Then: "*Oy gevalt!*" Then the question: "Is he Jewish?"

Sadistically, I paused several seconds before answering her. "Yes, Mom. He's Jewish."

Total silence. I couldn't even detect any breathing.

"Mom, are you still there?"

"Yes, of course, Renee, I'm here. When isn't your mother here? I'm just a little speechless with surprise. A daughter calls me up out of the blue, I don't even know she's going with someone. How *should* I know? So I'm surprised."

"Aren't you happy? Isn't this what you always wanted?"

"Yes, of course I'm happy. Of course this is what I always wanted."

But she didn't sound all that happy. All that anxiety over whether and whom I would marry should, one might have thought, have made this moment one of great jubilation. A giant hosanna ought to be swelling out of the phone. I had pictured my mother—a little woman, barely five feet tall, dark and very thin, for she can't eat when she's worried, which means she averages maybe one good meal a week—bursting out into *Hallel*, the song to praise God, in which He is called by every good name in the Hebrew vocabulary. How had I failed her this time? What maternal expectations was I once again in the process of thwarting?

And then I understood, saw it as I had never seen it before. My mother's whole life is devoted to worry. In the last few years she had been consumed in despair about two things: Would my brother's wife, Tzippy, who had been trying to have a child for two years, never succeed? And would her prodigal daughter, Renee, remain forever single, or worse, marry a *goy*? These were big, satisfying worries, requiring constant attention.

Then a few weeks ago she had learned that Tzippy was pregnant, and now I was calling to tell her that I'm marrying. A Jew yet. No wonder she sounded wounded. We children had callously deprived her life of its substance and meaning. She was holding the telephone receiver and staring down into the existential abyss.

"Of course I'm happy," she repeated weakly. "Overjoyed. Tell me, what is the young man like? What does he do? Don't tell me, he's also a philosopher." Do tell me, do tell me, her voice was begging.

"He's a mathematician."

"A mathematician? From numbers he makes a living?" Her voice gathered some strength.

"Yes, Mom. He's famous. He's one of the greatest living mathematicians. He's a genius. He was written up in *Life* magazine . . ."

"Really? A famous genius? *Life* magazine? This is really something then. This is real *Yiches*." (*Yiches* is prestige.) "You should be very proud, Renee, that such a man should love you. Of course, I know you're not just any girl. Who should know if not me? This is why God gave you such good brains, so that you could make such a man like this love you. I only wish your father were alive today to hear such news."

REBECCA GOLDSTEIN, *The Mind-Body Problem*

How sweet is your love,
My own, my bride!
How much more delightful your love than wine,
Your ointments more fragrant
Than any spice!
Sweetness drops
From your lips, O bride;

Honey and milk
Are under your tongue;
And the scent of your robes
Is like the scent of Lebanon . . .

Let me be a seal upon your heart,
Like the seal upon your hand.
For love is fierce as death,
Passion is mighty as Sheol;
Its darts are darts of fire,
A blazing flame.
Vast floods cannot quench love,
Nor rivers drown it.
If a man offered all his wealth for love,
He would be laughed to scorn.
SONG OF SONGS 8:6–7

Rachel Samstat's Jewish Prince Routine

You know what a Jewish prince is, don't you?
   (*Cocks her eyebrow*)
If you don't, there's an easy way to recognize one. A simple
sentence. "Where's the butter?"
   (*A long pause here, because the laugh starts slowly and
   builds*)
Okay. We all know where the butter is, don't we?
   (*A little smile*)
The butter is in the refrigerator.
   (*Beat*)
The butter is in the refrigerator in the little compartment in the
door marked "Butter."
   (*Beat*)
But the Jewish prince doesn't mean "Where's the butter?" He

means "Get me the butter." He's too clever to say "Get me" so he says "Where's."

(Beat)

And if you say to him—

(Shouting)

"in the refrigerator"—

(Resume normal voice)

and he goes to look, an interesting thing happens, a medical phenomenon that has not been sufficiently remarked upon.

(Beat)

The effect of the refrigerator light on the male cornea.

(Beat)

Blindness.

(A long beat)

"I don't see it anywhere."

(Pause)

"Where's the butter" is only one of the ways the Jewish prince reveals himself. Sometimes he puts it a different way. He says, "Is there any butter?"

(Beat)

We all know whose fault it is if there isn't, don't we?

(Beat)

When he's being really ingenious, he puts it in a way that's meant to sound as if what he needs most of all from you is your incredible wisdom and judgment and creativity. He says, "How do you think butter would taste with this?"

(Beat)

He's usually referring to dry toast.

(Beat)

I've always believed that the concept of the Jewish princess was invented by a Jewish prince who couldn't get his wife to fetch him the butter.

NORA EPHRON, *Heartburn*

Give your ear to all, your hand to your friends, but your lips only to your wife.

YIDDISH FOLK SAYING

I ask you, my friend, who started all this business of marriage and of wives?

SHOLOM ALEICHEM, *Gymnazie*

When he is late for dinner and I know he must be having an affair or lying dead in the street, I always hope he's dead.

JUDITH VIORST in Leo Rosten, *Carnival of Wit*

Since creation, God has engaged in making matches, a task as difficult as dividing the Red Sea.

GENESIS RABBAH 68:4

Politics don't make strange bedfellows, marriage does.

GROUCHO MARX

Two who quarrel constantly should not marry one another.

TALMUD: KIDDUSHIN

Men often marry their mothers.

EDNA FERBER

A man should never force himself upon his wife and never overpower her, for the Divine Spirit never rests upon one whose conjugal relations occur in the absence of desire, love, and free will.

MOSES BEN NAHMAN, *The Holy Letter*

Isaac mourned his mother Sarah for three years. At the end of those years he married Rebecca and stopped mourning his mother.

Thus we see that until a man takes a wife, he directs his love toward his parent. Once he marries, he directs his love toward his wife.

PIRKEI DE-RABBI ELIEZER 32

There was once a pious man who was married to a pious woman, and they did not have any children.

They said, "We are of no use to God," and they divorced one another.

The man went and married a wicked woman, and she made him wicked.

The woman went and married a wicked man, and she made him good.

This proves that all depends on the woman.

GENESIS RABBAH 17:7

THE MARRIAGE JESTER'S SONG

S. J. Agnon

Hurrah hurrah, let us all be glad
Now that the bridegroom has come to Brod.

Up wi' you players, and take your tools,
Fiddle and don't stand there like fools.

Start up a tune and bang the drum
Now that the bridegroom to town has come.

Shout out loud, burst into song,
And the whole town will come and dance in the throng.

And you brethren without a care,
Clap your hands to honor the pair.

Beloved and pleasant as in tales of yore,
Mistress Pessele and Reb Sheftel Shor,

And in honor of his father by all men discerned,
Our wealthy Master Reb Vovi the learned,

And in honor of the father known to us each one,
Namely the Hassid Reb Yudel Nathanson,

And in honor of their wives whose names I don't know,
And of families and those who have come for the show

From all the world over, from Brod and Rohatin
May they enjoy themselves for ever with their kin.
from *The Bridal Canopy*

I would say that the sexual organs express the human soul more than any other part of the body. They are not diplomats. They tell the truth ruthlessly . . . They are even more *meshuga* than the brain.
ISAAC BASHEVIS SINGER, *Conversations*

The Bintel Brief ("Bundle of Letters") began appearing in The Forward *in 1906 when the editor, Abraham Cahan, decided to make the pages of his paper more vivid with real-life stories.*

I am a young man of twenty-one and would like to marry my seventeen-year-old cousin, but she's quite small and I happen to be quite tall. So when we walk down the street together, people look at us. Could this lead to an unpleasant life if we were to marry?

I am a young man of twenty-five, and I recently met a fine girl. She has a flaw, however—a dimple in her chin. It is said that people who have this lose their first husband or wife. I love her very much. But I'm afraid to marry her lest I die because of the dimple.

Answer: The tragedy is not that the girl has a dimple in her chin but that some people have a screw loose in their heads.

Therefore must the bride below have a canopy, all beautiful with decorations prepared for her, in order to honor the Bride above, who comes to be present and participate in the joy of the bride below. For this reason it is necessary that the canopy be as beautiful as possible, and the Supernal Bride be invited to come and share in the joy.

ZOHAR

FAMILY, CHILDREN, AGING, AND PEACE

*I*N MY CHILDREN'S VERNACULAR, ours is an "amazing" family. There is no standard by which one measures "amazingness." For me, it is a state of feeling genuinely blessed, loved, and supported by many family members. I have a mother, stepfather, brother, two sisters, three sisters-in-law, four brothers-in-law, two parents-in-law, at this counting eighteen nieces and nephews, and one incredible matriarchal grandmother, pushing ninety. Naturally, there are many aunts, uncles, and cousins—too numerous to name, not to mention the very close friends who truly feel like family to me. Most important, I am blessed with four wonderful daughters and a husband whom I love. I feel lucky. Do I feel lucky every day? No—of course not. That's human nature. At times it can be overwhelming. My almost daily fantasies of a one-way ticket to a remote town in Italy are testament to the mixed blessings of a huge close-knit clan. I complain on a regular basis about the meals; the shopping for food, clothes, gifts, school supplies; the visits; and the daunting number of holidays in the Jewish calendar. I clean and cook with the phone permanently affixed as I talk to guidance counselors, school nurses, countless relatives, and colleagues. And the labor is the easy part. It eats time and saps energy, but it pales against the psychological drama of family dynamics.

The family forms and defines us. Within its borders, our principles, ethics, self-worth, and aspirations blossom or wither. Parents seek to replicate or refashion their own upbringing, hoping only for the best. But the best differs for each of us. I have only to look at my four girls, each with her own singular beauty, talents, and traits, to know that there is no one way to love and nurture. Our home is a hothouse, and each flower has its needs.

In ninth grade, our Bible class spent the entire year studying and analyzing the families in Genesis with an emphasis on the sibling relationships and rivalries. Cain was jealous enough of Abel to kill him; the two half brothers, Isaac and Ishmael, fought over their father, Abraham's love, and Jacob lured Esau into the birthright sale and deceived his father, Isaac. Certainly there must have been many problems among Jacob's children—there were twelve of them, after all. His gift to Joseph of the multicolored coat and the jealousy it engendered is merely the best-known incident. Our biblical forefathers are presented to us, warts and all—because the message is not to deny human nature but to overcome its darker side.

When a father gives to his son, both laugh. When a son gives to his father, both cry.
YIDDISH PROVERB

Aging, the challenge and the fear of it, pervades our world in ways our forefathers could not conceive. With advances in medicine, people are living much longer. My remarkable great-aunt is eighty-four years old, works full-time, and carries in her wallet the following prescription from her doctor: "Keep working." Not many older people are that fortunate. They are often vulnerable in our competitive, fast-paced, youth-obsessed society. Aging requires grace—the revolutions in cosmetic surgery are besides the point. With a little compassion, we can help them and, in the process, gain a great deal.

There is a story in the Talmud (Moed 23a) of a righteous man who journeyed on a road and stopped when he saw a man planting a carob tree. He asked him, "How long does it take for this tree you are planting to bear fruit?" The man, who was working busily, stopped and said, "Seventy years." The traveler further asked him if he was certain that he would live for another seventy years, and the man replied, "I found ready-grown carob trees in the world; as my forefathers planted these for me so I too plant these for my children."

As parents all we can do is plant the right trees and hope for the best. Our sages offer rules on child rearing, our geriatricians provide guidelines on aging parents, our humorists and pundits comfort us with their stories. As we struggle to understand and shape our own family experiences, we need all the advice we can get.

Then God blessed them [Adam and Eve] and said: Be fruitful and multiply and fill the earth.
GENESIS 1:28

Train up a child in the way he should go, and when he is old, he will not depart from it.
PROVERBS 22:6

The following poem is based on the biblical story of Sarah who gave birth to her first child, Isaac, at the age of ninety-nine. (Genesis 21)

SARAH

Delmore Schwartz

The angel said to me: "Why are you laughing?"
"Laughing! Not me. Who was laughing? I did not laugh. It
    was
A cough. I was coughing. Only hyenas laugh.
It was the cold I caught nine minutes after
Abraham married me: when I saw
How I was slender and beautiful, more and more
Slender and beautiful.
I was also
Clearing my throat; something inside of me
Is continually telling me something
I do not wish to hear: A joke: A big joke:
But the joke is always just on me.
He said: you will have more children than the sky's stars
Wait: patiently: ninety years? You see
The joke's on me!"

Immediately on our arrival in Hamburg, I became with child, and my mother along with me. In good time the Lord graciously delivered me of a young daughter. I was still a mere girl, and unused as I was to bearing children, it naturally went hard with me; yet I rejoiced mightily that the Most High had bestowed on me a healthy, lovely baby. My good mother had reckoned out her time for the same day. However, she had great joy in my being brought to bed first, so she could help me a little, young girl that I was. Eight days later my mother likewise brought forth a young daughter in childbirth. So there was neither envy nor reproach between us, and we lay next to each other in the same room. But, Lord, we had no peace, for the people that came running in to see the marvel, a mother and daughter together in childbed.

GLUCKEL OF HAMELN, *The Memoirs of Glukel of Hameln*

I grew up to have my father's looks—my father's speech patterns—my father's posture—my father's walk—my father's opinions—and my mother's contempt for my father.

JULES FEIFFER

Whoever brings up an orphan in his home is regarded by the Bible as though the child has been born to him.

TALMUD: SANHEDRIN 19b

There are children playing in the street who could solve some of my top problems in physics because they have modes of sensory perception that I lost long ago.

J. ROBERT OPPENHEIMER

How good and how pleasant it is that brothers sit together.

PSALM 133

A man should never single out one of his children for favored treatment for because of two extra coins' worth of silk, which Jacob gave to Joseph and not to his other sons; Joseph's brothers became jealous of him, and one thing led to another until our ancestors became slaves in Egypt.

TALMUD: SHABBAT 10b

The best security for old age: respect your children.

SHOLEM ASCH

When the people of Israel stood at Mount Sinai ready to receive the Torah, God said to them, "Bring me good securities to guarantee that you will keep it, and then I will give the Torah to you."

They said, "Our ancestors will be our securities."
Said God to them, "I have faults to find with your ancestors . . . But bring Me good securities and I will give it to you."
They said, "King of the Universe, our prophets will be our securities."
He replied, "I have faults to find with your prophets . . . Still, bring Me good securities and I will give the Torah to you."
They said to him, "Our children will be our securities."

And God replied, "Indeed these are good securities. For their sake I will give you the Torah."
Hence it is written: "Out of the mouth of babes and sucklings You have founded strength."
Song of Songs Rabbah 1:4

Small children interfere with your sleep, big children your life.
Yiddish proverb

You don't know how much you don't know until your children grow up and tell you how much you don't know.
S. J. Perelman

There were two brothers who were farmers. One lived with his wife and children on one side of a hill, and the other, unmarried, lived in a small hut on the other side of the hill.

One year the brothers had an especially good harvest. The married brother looked over his fields and thought to himself: "God has been so good to me. I have a wife and children, and more crops than I need. I am so much better off than my brother, who lives all alone. Tonight while my brother sleeps, I will carry some of my sheaves to his field. When he finds them tomorrow he'll never suspect that they came from me."

On the other side of the hill, the unmarried brother looked at his harvest and thought to himself: "God has been kind to me. But I wish He had been as good to my brother. His needs are so much greater than mine. He must feed his wife and children, yet I have as much fruit and grain as he does. Tonight, while my brother and his family sleep, I will place some of my sheaves in his field. Tomorrow, when he finds them, he will never know that I have less and he has more."

So both brothers waited patiently until midnight. Then each loaded his grain on his shoulders and walked toward the top of the hill. Exactly at midnight, they met one another at the hilltop. Realizing that each had thought only of helping the other, they embraced and cried with joy.

FRANCINE KLAGSBRUN, *Voices of Wisdom*

Happiness is having a large, loving, caring, close-knit family in another city.

GEORGE BURNS

A person should not promise to give a child something and then not give it, because in that way the child learns to lie.

TALMUD: SUKKAH 46b

I know this will sound absurd to some grown-ups, but when I talk with children about their daydreams and fantasies, about heaven, about animals and other gentle aspects of their yearnings, I'm not asking these questions as an ingenious interviewer. I'm asking because I really want to know the answer. Sometimes I feel I almost conspire with children to imagine a better world than the one we're stuck with.

JONATHAN KOZOL in *New Menorah* 44 (Summer 1996)

Frau Frumet Wolf lived at the end of the eighteenth century and is a rare example of a bold woman. She wrote anonymous controversial pamphlets concerning issues in the Jewish community. The following is the will she left for her children:

I wanted, on the occasion of my farewell, to leave you, my dear children, instructions and rules for conduct. As all of you, however, are grown up, I cannot advise you as is usual with minors. I shall therefore limit myself to some general though important instructions.

Above all I admonish you to cherish virtue and fear God; otherwise you can neither achieve full happiness on earth nor find peace and reward in the world to come. Content yourself with your fate and fortune and accommodate your needs to your income, behave peacefully to everybody and among yourselves. Do not allow yourselves to become involved in harmful family conflicts. Live, moreover, in concord and assist each other with advice and deeds . . .

from *Written Out of History*, ed. Sondra Henry and Emily Taitz

Children are my best readers, I only wish adults should behave in the same way. A child loves a story, you cannot give to a child a book without a story. He is an independent reader, he is not influenced by reviews because children do not read reviews. He is not influenced by authorities, you can tell a child God Almighty himself wrote a book and if the child does not like it he will reject it. Where do you get among adults such readers nowadays?

ISAAC BASHEVIS SINGER, *Conversations*

I often feel that the children I meet even in the poorest places have a spiritual cleanness about them that makes them seem like messengers from somewhere else. Even when children are surrounded by enormous suffering and sickness, their capacity to affirm life in the midst of death is a miracle that refreshes the world. Someone, I don't know who, once said, "If you seek God, look for a child." I've been looking for God in the faces of children for thirty years.

JONATHAN KOZOL in *New Menorah* 44 (Summer 1996)

The Genius

In a recent article, "Are Writers Born?" I said that while geniuses may be born, they are few and far between. Writing requires hard work. After reading this, a charming housewife in Brooklyn wrote to say that her little boy, age nine, was normal, although he did show flashes of being pretty smart. On "Parents Day" she visited the class. All the kids were singing or reading but her little boy was going around picking up a piece of paper, scrutinizing the bottom of a chair, dusting erasers, cleaning a table, and the mother immediately wondered how such genius went unnoticed.

She was barely able to conceal her excitement when she approached the teacher after the session. The mother wildly tried to think of words to inform the teacher tactfully about the hidden jewel, her son, who was picked to do the scrutinizing. The mother said, "Miss Clark, does Robert always wander about the classroom while you teach?" The teacher replied, "Only when he's janitor for the day."

HARRY GOLDEN, *You're Entitle'*

Your own offspring teaches you reason.

TALMUD: YEBAMOTH 63

And you shall teach them diligently to your children — these are your students.

SIFRE ON DEVARIM 6:7

I can understand why we can't have a Jewish President. It would be embarrassing to hear the President's mother screaming Love at the grandchildren: "Who's Grandma's baby? Who's Grandma's baby?"
LENNY BRUCE, *How to Talk Dirty and Influence People*

A young scholar of Chelm, innocent in the ways of earthly matters, was stunned one morning when his wife gave birth. Pell-mell he ran to the rabbi.

"Rabbi," he blurted out, "an extraordinary thing has happened! Please explain it to me! My wife has just given birth although we have been married only three months! How can this be? Everybody knows it takes nine months for a baby to be born!"

The rabbi, a world-renowned sage, put on his silver-rimmed spectacles and furrowed his brow reflectively.

"My son," he said, "I see you haven't the slightest idea about such matters, nor can you make the simplest calculation. Let me ask you: Have you lived with your wife three months?"

"Yes."

"Has she lived with you three months?"

"Yes."

"Together—have you lived three months?"

"Yes."

"What's the total then—three months plus three plus three?"

"Nine months, Rabbi!"

"Then why do you come to bother me with your foolish questions!"

from *A Treasury of Jewish Folklore*, ed. Nathan Ausubel

By the time your son is old enough not to be ashamed of you, his own son is already ashamed of him.
SAM LEVENSON, *You Don't Have to Be in Who's Who to Know What's What*

Somewhere on this globe, every ten seconds, there is a woman giving birth to a child. She must be found and stopped!
SAM LEVENSON, *You Don't Have to Be in Who's Who to Know What's What*

One is conditioned early in family life to an interpretation of the world. And the grieving is that no matter how much happiness or success you collect, you cannot obliterate your early experience — diminished perhaps, it stays with you.
BERNARD MALAMUD, *Conversations*

My mother was dead for five years before I knew that I loved her very much.
LILLIAN HELLMAN, *An Unfinished Woman*

A brother who has been offended [becomes more inaccessible] than a strong city, and quarrels separate more than the bolt of a castle.
PROVERBS 25:18, 19

Adam was the luckiest man: he had no mother-in-law.
SHOLOM ALEICHEM

Yussel and his father sat in the kitchen of the split-level. It was Yussel's Hanukah visit. His father was wearing his silk pajamas. He had two luxuries: silk pajamas and Zabar's French Roast. He had two pairs of maroon silk pajamas, walked around in them, looked more like a king in those pajamas than in his clothes, explained he should sleep in silk because if his soul were to travel at night, his soul should go up to the higher rungs clothed in silk. He did not consider his pajamas a luxury. His father had taken another loan out on the split-level to give money for somebody's sister's operation. He couldn't remember who. Yussel wrote another check. It was the fourteenth time he'd paid off the mortgage. His father made coffee. The kitchen was filthy. His mother had a headache. Yussel was still arguing with his father that he should take out life insurance. His father was still refusing.

"If I tell my people I'm going to die, they'll explode. They'll start early with their craziness. And your mother, she'll start early to sell my clothes to raise cash for the funeral. All that herring, all those hard-boiled eggs. Why should my last days be spent naked surrounded by shmegeggies already wearing my old clothes?"

Yussel laughed. "She'll rent your room."

His father nodded. "She'll rent my room before I die. She'll bake strudel for the shiva and not give me a bite."

"She'll fly everyone out from New York thirty days early on SuperSaver."

The Rabbi and Yussel hugged each other, tears of laughter sparkled on their beards. "I'll be naked, sitting on the sidewalk while the Salvation Army truck carries my bed from the house."

They held each other, like bears, Yussel great and hairy, his father small and fiery, and danced with each other into the dining room, around the living room. In the living room, his father stopped, held Yussel at arm's length, searched his face as if he were seeing it for the first time. "Yussele. Tottele." His voice was low. "I know you won't attach to HaShem. Believe me, I understand your reasons. But when you smile like this, Yussele, I see Him in your eyes. I see all the generations before you. You can't hide your heart, Yussele. You can try but you can't hide your heart. Deny it if you want, but someone will see it, someone will figure you out. . . ."

RHODA LERMAN, *God's Ear*

My Pop was a tailor, and sometimes he made as much as eighteen dollars a week. But he was no ordinary tailor. His record as the most inept tailor that Yorkville ever produced has never been approached. This could even include parts of Brooklyn and the Bronx.

The notion that Pop was a tailor was an opinion that was held only by him. To his customers he was known as "Misfit Sam." He was the only tailor I ever heard of who refused to use a tape measure. A tape measure might be all right for an undertaker, he maintained, but not for a tailor who had the unerring eye of an eagle. He insisted that a tape measure was pure swank and utter nonsense, adding that if a tailor had to measure a man he couldn't be much of a tailor in the first place. Pop boasted that he could size up a man just by looking at him, and turn out a perfect fit. The results of his appraisals were about as accurate as Chamberlain's predictions about Hitler.

Our neighborhood was full of Pop's customers. They were easily recognizable in the street, for they all walked around with one trouser leg shorter than the other, one sleeve longer than the other or coat collars undecided where to rest. The inevitable result was that my father never had the same customers twice. This meant that he had to be constantly on the prowl for new business, and as our neighborhood became more populated with gents in misfit clothing, he had to find locations where his reputation had not preceded him. He roamed far and wide — Hoboken, Passaic, Nyack and beyond. As his reputation grew, he was forced to go farther and farther from the home base to snare new victims. Many weeks his carfare was larger than his income. And his corns and bunions, tended by one of my favorite uncles, the talented Dr. Krinkler, were bigger than both of them.

GROUCHO MARX, *Groucho and Me*

When I hear she's coming to stay with us, I'm pleased. I think of "grandmother" as a generic brand. My friends have grandmothers who seem permanently bent over cookie racks. They are Nanas and Bubbas, sources of constant treats, huggers and kissers, pinchers of cheeks.

I have no memory of my own grandmother, who has lived in a distant state, and whom I haven't seen since I was a baby. But, with the example of the neighborhood grandmothers before me, I can hardly wait to have a grandmother of my own—and the cookies will be nice, too. For, while my uncles provide a cuisine that ranges from tuna croquettes to Swedish meatballs, they show no signs of baking anything more elegant than a potato.

My main concern on the day of my grandmother's arrival is, How soon will she start the cookies?

. . . She pats my head—a good sign—and asks me to sing the Israeli national anthem. I have the impression that I am auditioning for her, and I am. I sing "Hatikvah" (off key, but she can't quite hear me), and she gives me a dollar: a wonderful start.

Uncles Len and Gabe go off to their respective jobs, leaving me alone with Etka from Minsk for the first time. I look at her, expecting her to toss off her tailored jacket, tuck up her cuffs, and roll out the cookie dough. Instead, she purses her lips in an expression she learned as a child, and tilts her head in a practiced way: "Now, perhaps, you could fix me a little lunch?"

LAURA CUNNINGHAM, *Sleeping Arrangements*

Let us be grateful to our parents: had they not been tempted, we would not be here.

TALMUD: ABODAH ZARAH, 5a

Honor your father and mother, even as you honor God; for all three were partners in your creation.

ZOHAR

After a certain age, the more one becomes oneself, the more obvious one's family traits become.

MARCEL PROUST, *Remembrance of Things Past*

Parents can only give good advice or put them in the right paths, but the final forming of a person's character lies in their own hands.

ANNE FRANK, *The Dairy of a Young Girl*, 15 July 1944

My husband tells me that there are always a few old men in the synagogue who weep silently when they recite this haunting prayer on Yom Kippur:

Do not cast me off in old age;
when my strength fails me, do not forsake me!

PSALM 71:9

The test of a people is how it behaves toward the old. It is easy to love children. Even tyrants and dictators make a point of being fond of children. But affection and care for the old, the incurable, the helpless, are the true gold mines of a culture.

ABRAHAM HESCHEL, *The Insecurity of Freedom*

What good is it to turn fifty with an unwrinkled face if there's no light behind the eyes, no passion in the voice, no new ideas happening inside the head? Why hope to live a long life if we're only going to fill it with self-absorption, body maintenance, and image repair? When we die, do we want people to exclaim, "She looked ten years younger," or do we want them to say, "She lived a great life?"

LETTY COTTIN POGREBIN, *Getting Over Getting Older*

One ought to enter old age the way one enters the senior year at a university, in exciting anticipation of consummation. Rich in perspective, experienced in failure, the person advanced in years is capable of shedding prejudices and the fever of vested interests. He does not see anymore in every fellow man a person who stands in his way, and competitiveness may cease to be his way of thinking.

ABRAHAM HESCHEL, *The Insecurity of Freedom*

THE FIRST GRAY HAIR
Yehudah Halevi

One day I saw a gray hair in my head;
I plucked it out when thus to me it said:
"Think, if thou wilt, that thou art rid of me,
I've twenty friends who soon will mock at thee."
from *A Treasury of Jewish Humor*, ed. Nathan Ausubel

Reverence for the old, dialogue between generations, is as important to the dignity of the young as it is for the well-being of the old. We deprive ourselves by disparaging the old.

ABRAHAM HESCHEL, *The Insecurity of Freedom*

The family is a paradigm of our relationship with the outside world. If we can make sense of one, we are better equipped to deal with the other, better equipped to find happiness and spread it. Society needs all the peacemakers it can produce. Our planet, our people, and our survival depend on the minds we first seek to nourish in our homes. It's for this reason that I chose to conclude this section with thoughts on peace. If we can make a few compromises at the dinner table, can global harmony be far away?

First a person should put his house together, then his town, then the world.

RABBI ISRAEL SALANTER

And they shall beat their swords into plowshares and their spears into pruning hooks. Nation shall not lift up sword against nation, neither shall they learn war anymore.

ISAIAH 2:4

Have we not one father, hath not one God created us, wherefore shall we deal treacherously with each other?

MALACHI 2:10

By virtue of three things does the world endure: truth, justice and peace.

Ethics of the Fathers 1:18

Rejoice not when thine enemy falleth, And let not thy heart be glad when he stumbleth.

PROVERBS 24:17

But the humble shall inherit the land, And delight themselves in the abundance of peace.

PSALM 37:11

It is not your obligation to complete the task [of perfecting the world], but neither are you free to desist from doing all you can.

Ethics of the Fathers 2:21

Hillel says: Be among the disciples of Aaron, loving peace and pursuing peace, loving people, and bringing them closer to the Torah.

Ethics of the Fathers 1:12

In the Bible, Moses' brother, Aaron, is considered a lover of peace to the point where he allowed a small lie now and then to resolve conflict:

When two men had quarreled, Aaron would go and sit with one of them and say, "My son, see what your friend is doing! He beats his breast and tears his clothes and moans, 'Woe is me! How can I lift my eyes and look my companion in the face? I am ashamed before him, since it is I who treated him foully.' "

Aaron would sit with him until he had removed all anger from his heart.

Then Aaron would go and sit with the other man and say likewise, "My son, see what your friend is doing! He beats his breast and tears his clothes and moans, 'Woe is me! How can I lift my eyes and look my companion in the face? I am ashamed before him.' "

Aaron would sit with him also until he had removed all anger from his heart.

Later, when the two met, they would embrace and kiss each other.

Avot de Rabbi Nathan

A leader who doesn't hesitate before he sends his nation into battle is not fit to be a leader.

Golda Meir in Joseph Telushkin, *Jewish Wisdom*

If you see in a province oppression of the poor and suppression of right and justice, don't wonder at the fact; for one high official is protected by a higher one, and both of them by still higher ones.

Ecclesiastes 5:7

The whole of the Torah is for promoting peace, as it is written, "Her ways are pleasant, and all her paths peaceful."

Talmud: Gitten 59b

Even on the threshold of war, we [Jews] are bidden to begin in no other way than with peace, for it is written: "When you draw near a city to fight, first offer it peace."
MIDRASH: LEVITICUS RABBAH

When anyone in power thinks he knows the truth—thinks he can attain the ideal state for mankind—it leads to war. It's better to recognize that man can never be perfect. At best, he is an aspiring beast and must be controlled. Democracy and freedom of ideas work best as long as we can never be sure what the truth is.
PADDY CHAYEFSKY in the *New York Post*, March 2, 1962

As the leader, so the generation.
TALMUD: ARAKIN 17a

We all love the same children, weep the same tears, hate the same enmity, and pray for reconciliation. Peace has no borders.
YITZHAK RABIN in a 1995 interview while visiting New York City

Better a morsel of dry bread, and peace with it, than a house full of feasting, with strife.
FOLK SAYING

He who makes peace in heaven, May He make peace over us and all Israel. Amen.

Upon the laws it was unnecessary to expatiate. A glance at them showed that they teach not impiety, but the most genuine piety; that they invite men not to hate their fellows, but to share their possessions; that they are foes of injustice and scrupulous for justice, banish sloth and extravagance, and teach men to be self-dependent and to work with a will; that they deter them from war for the sake of conquest, but render them valiant defenders of the laws themselves . . .

What more beneficial than to be in harmony with one another?

JOSEPHUS, *Against Apion* II

This is what our most holy prophet through all his regulations, especially desires to create, unanimity, neighbourliness, fellowship, reciprocity of feeling, whereby houses and cities and nations and countries and the whole human race may advance to supreme happiness.

PHILO, *The Special Laws*

There is no doubt whatsoever in my mind that the risks of peace are preferable by far to the grim certainties that await every nation in war.

YITZHAK RABIN

How beautiful upon the mountains are the feet of the messenger of good tidings, that announces peace!

ISAIAH 52:7

When a man has made peace within himself, he will be able to make peace in the whole world.

MARTIN BUBER, *The Way of Man*

THE SABBATH
AND THE HOLIDAYS

*H*OLIDAYS AND RITUALS FILL the Jewish calendar commemorating the formative events of our ancient history. They are enjoyed and appreciated at many different levels by all Jews. Whether one is observant and attends synagogue regularly, attends a service just on the high holy days, or only participates in an occasional Sabbath dinner or Passover Seder, these events and celebrations tap a wellspring of emotions and memories that often takes the celebrant by surprise. Sights, sounds, and tastes contribute to the experience. Sometimes the memories are created around the melodies of certain prayers, the haunting sounds of the shofar on Rosh Hashannah or the noisy groggers on Purim. Jews consecrate and perpetuate the indelible images of own history with religious ceremonies like blowing the shofar, blessing the lulav and etrog on Sukkot, dancing with Torahs on Simchat Torah, and lighting the candles on the eight nights of Hanukkah.

Long before Proust tasted the madeleine which inspired his life's literary work, the specific foods we have tasted, smelled, or prepared for the Jewish holidays—honey and round challahs on Rosh Hashannah, latkes on Hanukkah, charoset on Passover, and blintzes on Shavuoth—evoked comforting memories of things past. These memories transport us to distant times and places and comfort us with the knowledge that there is continuity and meaning in our lives.

When I was a child, the Sabbath began at sundown with a walk down an elm-shaded suburban street to the local Orthodox synagogue. I would hold my father's hand all the while, annoyed that my sister and I would probably be the only girls in the synagogue. But my father said that women were not exempt from prayer.

My mother was a professor who hated to cook and my father was "into" health before it was fashionable. Artichokes and cottage cheese are not exactly one's idea of a Friday night Shabbos meal, but unless my paternal grandmother was visiting and taking over the kitchen, there was nothing on our table that resembled gefilte fish, chicken soup, flanken, or brisket — the delicacies served in my friends' homes. What made Friday night special was that we were together as a family. My mother lit the candles, my father made the blessing over the wine and the challahs. (Recently, I was happy to learn that women are permitted to recite the kiddush and now either one of my four daughters or I perform it.)

Toward the end of the meal, we would study one or two verses of *Ethics of the Fathers* and sing Sabbath songs. We had a ritual of going around the table and each person was required to select a song. Just as we didn't have a traditional menu, the menu of song selections was equally eclectic — it didn't have to be Hebrew, just a song. It was particularly amusing when we had a guest who was also required to pick a song, which usually meant no matter how the person sang, my siblings and I couldn't look at each other lest we burst out uncontrollably with laughter. It's a funny thing about memory. I recall perfectly the slight irritation I often felt, chafing to get away from the table and back to my book or a good game of Scrabble with one of my siblings. On a deeper level, it is the warmth and laughter that really stay with me — that weekly legacy of a family gathering together, everything else on hold. I try to remember that when I watch my own daughters, squirming with the same impatience at our table. Homework, friends, and entertainment can wait. It's Friday night . . .

Hashem [the Lord] spoke to Moses, saying: Speak to the Children of Israel and say to them: Hashem's appointed festivals that you are to designate as holy convocations — these are My appointed festivals. For six days labor may be done, and the seventh day is a day of complete rest, a holy convocation, you shall not do any work; it is a Sabbath for Hashem in all your dwelling places.

LEVITICUS 23:1–4

He who delights in the Sabbath is granted his heart's desires.

TALMUD: SHABBAT 118b

The Sabbath menu that brings delight: a dish of beets, a large fish and heads of garlic.

TALMUD: SHABBAT 118b

An individual must please his wife on the Sabbath with endearing words.

ZOHAR

Wherefore the children of Israel shall keep the Sabbath to observe the Sabbath throughout the generations for a perpetual covenant.

EXODUS 31:16

When the body is laboring the soul may be at rest and when
the body is enjoying relaxation, the soul may be laboring.
PHILO, *On the Festivals* 3:270

Call the Sabbath a delight . . . and thou shalt honor it.
ISAIAH 58:13

*Maybe it was the benches by the lake with the sun setting over
the mountains and the congregation of campers all out of shorts
and T-shirts, looking their Friday night best, but at Camps Massad and Ramah, this poem was sung in Hebrew on Friday nights
with one of the most beautiful melodies I know.*

QUEEN SABBATH
Chaim Nachman Bialik

The sun on the tree-tops no longer is seen,
So let us wend forth to welcome the Queen.
The Sabbath is coming, the holy, the blessed,
And with her troop of angels of peace and of rest.
Come, O come to us, dear Queen!
Come, O come to us, dear Queen!
Peace unto you, O angels of peace!

We've welcomed the Sabbath with songs and with praise;
With joy in our hearts now wend homeward our ways.
The table is set and the candles alight,
At home every corner is sparkling and bright.
Sabbath blessings, Sabbath peace!
Sabbath blessings, Sabbath peace!
O come you in peace, you angels of peace!

O stay with us, pure one! We'll bask in your glow
A night and a day, and then you will go.

We'll wear our best clothes to honor the day;
Three times we will feast, and we'll sing and we'll pray,
In perfection of our rest,
In the pleasantest of rest.
O bless us with peace, you angels of peace!

The sun on the tree-tops no longer is seen,
So we'll go bid farewell to Sabbath the Queen,
O pure one, O holy, in peace shall you go,
Six days we'll await your return, as you know,
Till Sabbath Queen comes again!
Till Sabbath Queen comes again!
Depart you in peace, you angels of peace!

He who feels in his heart a genuine tie with the life of his people cannot possibly conceive of the existence of the Jewish people apart from "Queen Sabbath." We can say without exaggeration that more than Israel preserved the Sabbath, the Sabbath preserved Israel.

ACHAD HA'AM, *At the Crossroads*

It was the darkness and emptiness of the streets I liked most about Friday evening, as if in preparation for that day of rest and worship which the Jews greet "as a bride" — that day when the very touch of money is prohibited, all work, all travel, all household duties, even to the turning on and off of a light — Jewry had found its way past its tormented heart to some ancient still center of itself. I waited for the streets to go dark on Friday evening as other children waited for the Christmas lights. Even Friday morning after the tests were over glowed in anticipation. When I returned home after three, the warm odor of a coffee cake baking in the oven and the sight of my mother on her hands and knees scrubbing the linoleum on the dining room floor filled me with such tenderness that I could feel my senses reaching out to embrace every single object in our household. One Friday, after a morning in school spent on the voyages of Henry Hudson, I returned with the phrase "Among the discoverers of the New World" singing in my mind as the theme of my own newfound freedom on the Sabbath.

ALFRED KAZIN, A *Walker in the City*

Gedali

On Sabbath eves I am oppressed by the dense melancholy of memories. In bygone days on these occasions my grandfather would stroke the volumes of Ibn Ezra with his yellow beard. His old woman in her lace cap would trace fortunes with her knotty fingers over the Sabbath candles, and sob softly to herself. On those evenings my child's heart was rocked like a little ship upon enchanted waves. O the rotted Talmuds of my childhood! O the dense melancholy of memories!

I roam through Zhitomer in search of a shy star. By the ancient synagogue, by its yellow and indifferent walls, old Jews with prophets' beards and passionate rags on their sunken chests sell chalk and wicks and bluing.

Here before me is the market, and the death of the market. Gone is the fat of the soul of plenty. Dumb padlocks hang upon the booths, and the granite paving is as clean as a skull. My shy star blinks, and fades from sight.

Success came to me later on; success came just before sunset. Gedali's little shop was hidden away in a row of others, all hermetically closed. Where was your kindly shade that evening, Dickens? In that little old curiosity shop you would have seen gilt slippers, ship's cables, an ancient compass, a stuffed eagle, a Winchester with the date 1810 engraved upon it, a broken saucepan . . .

And then, from out of the blue gloom, the young Sabbath came to take her seat of honor.

"Gedali," I said, "today is Friday, and it's already evening. Where are Jewish biscuits to be got, and a Jewish glass of tea, and a little of that pensioned-off God in a glass of tea?" "Not to be had," Gedali replied, hanging the padlock on his little booth. "Not to be had. Next door is a tavern, and they were good people who served in it; but nobody eats there now, people weep there."

He buttoned his green frock coat on three bone buttons, flicked himself with the cock's feathers, sprinkled a little water on his soft palms, and departed, a tiny, lonely visionary in a black top hat, carrying a big prayerbook under his arm.

The Sabbath is coming. Gedali, the founder of an impossible International, has gone to the synagogue to pray.

ISAAC BABEL, *The Collected Stories of Isaac Babel*

The meaning of the Sabbath is to celebrate time rather than space. Six days a week we live under the tyranny of things of space; on the Sabbath we try to become attuned to holiness in time. It is a day when we are called upon to share in what is eternal in time, to turn from the results of creation to the creation of the world.

ABRAHAM HESCHEL, *The Sabbath*

First Snowfall in Chelm

One Friday afternoon the first snowfall came down on Chelm and the people rejoiced to see the clean white blanket covering the rutted streets and dingy houses of their city. But then they thought sadly: "The sexton will soon be passing through the town and call on the people to close their shops and prepare for the Sabbath. What will happen to the snow when he walks over it?"

Immediately the Rabbi and the seven worthies came together

to see what could be done. The snow, they decided, must at all costs be kept clean. But how will the merchants know when to close their shops for the Sabbath? They might, God forbid, violate the sanctity of the holy day! Finally the Rabbi issued an edict as follows:

"The sexton is to proclaim the Sabbath as usual. But he is not to go on foot. He is to stand up on a table and be carried through the town by four of the worthies."

from A *Treasury of Jewish Folklore*, ed. Nathan Ausubel

The Sabbath is the choicest fruit and flower of the week, the Queen whose coming changes the humblest home into a palace.

JUDAH HALEVI, *Kuzari*

The sun's scarcely begun to shine, and sweet summer's in the land, and folks have got so they are feeling newborn and glad-hearted, for seeing God's good earth looking fair again—well don't you know but that's just when our somber season sets in, and the time comes for Jews to start mourning and shedding tears in earnest. For it's then the whole roster of sad observances must be got through: the drear progression of fastings and self-denials and bewailments, lasting from the Numbering of Days, at winter's end and in the leafy prime of spring, 'twixt the Passover and the Feast-o'-Weeds, till well into the chill, drenching wet and muck of autumn. And it's then that, mind you, I, Reb Mendele the Book Peddler, have my work cut out and come into my own, making the circuit of Jewish towns with my cart-load of stock, from which I furnish the kindred with all the rueful necessaries of the rites of weeping—to wit: with Fastday lamentations and Penitential prayers, with Ladies' Breviaries and graveside recitals, with ram's horns and Festal Prayerbooks. So, there you are! Because, you see, whilst Jews are sorrowing everywhere and grieve the livelong summer away, wearing the season out with weeping, I do business and apply my living. But I've got off the point.

S. Y. ABRAMOVITSH,"Fishke the Lame," *Tales of Mendele the Book Peddler*

The rituals and disciplines that surrounded my childhood sensitized my spirit, made it permanently susceptible to the messages behind them; the names of the Patriarchs and the Kings and holy places were permanently lodged in me, and at a later period in my life reverberated again with those overtones which accompany and distinguish the essential nature of tradition.

MAURICE SAMUEL, *The Professor and the Fossil*

Passover is observed in the spring, usually during the month of April. It celebrates the Exodus and liberation of the Israelites from Egypt. The name is taken from the story in the Bible: During the last plague inflicted on Pharaoh to break his will, God passed over the homes of the Israelites and struck down only the Egyptian firstborn.

It seems to be the holiday most widely celebrated by Jews. Even the most secular of Jews usually harbors some special memory of the Passover seder. There is something about making or participating in a seder—and maybe even eating matzoh—that is essential in the ritualistic calendar of many Jews. Perhaps it has to do with springtime, with organizing, cleaning—a need for order and continuity.

The Exodus from Egypt occurs in every human being, in every era, in every year, and even in every day.

NACHMAN OF BRATSLAV

You shall rejoice in your festival, with your son and daughter
. . . the stranger, the fatherless and the widow in your communities.
DEUTERONOMY 16:14

*The theme of continuity is most clearly and simply expressed in
this passage from the Haggadah:*

In each generation every person is obliged to feel as though he
or she personally came out of Egypt.

Jews who have drifted from the faith of their fathers . . . are
stirred in their inmost parts when the old, familiar Passover
sounds chance to fall upon their ears.
HEINRICH HEINE, *Rabbi von Bacharach*

A Feather and a Wooden Spoon

Holidays! What can I tell you about holidays? Passover has always come upon me like an attack of malaria. For the early
symptoms, I clean cupboards, scrub floors and polish windows.
Later developments respond only to a full-blown cooking orgy.
I watch myself working like a madwoman but cannot stop. "Id-
iot! . . . Fool! Why must you carry on like this year after year?"
I ask myself while I hurry. But by the time I find the strength
to answer, the seder is ready—the guests are invited, the fish is
settled in the jelly broth, and the taiglakh heaped like marbles
in the honeyed glue . . .
    I saw Passover as a holiday of rapprochement between gen-
erations—not only the distant ones sojourning in Egypt, but the
closer ones wandering in modern deserts. Making Passover is my
message to *my* mother, who is no longer with us. "See Mama,
what a good daughter I am," is behind those sudden attacks of

domesticity. Polishing my father's silver wine cup—the one with his name and wedding date on it—kept his presence alive. Small gestures. Compensations. Tangles of guilt and affection.

There were other elements to contend with. When I was a little girl growing up in Williamsburg, the seasons didn't come and go as they pleased. My mother forced them to change. She turned off the summer by baking honey cakes for Rosh Hashana and warned the winter it was on its last legs by grinding poppy seeds for hamantashen. As soon as Purim was out of the way, she attacked the winter as if it were her worst enemy. She drove it off with brushes and brooms. Every piece of furniture was pulled from the wall to be sure that not a vestige of the dead season was trapped in the cobwebs. When there was no doubt that the winter was beaten, she made Pesach out of chicken fat, crates of eggs from a Lakewood farm, and matza from a special bakery where you could watch it slide out of the oven into your own box.

The frenzy of activity did not end until the evening before Passover. Then, my father went through the apartment with a feather, a candle, and a wooden spoon to exorcise the last invisible crumbs. I, myself, took the feather and spoon with me when I went off to school. Somewhere between home and P.S. 19 I would find an old crone warming her hands over a smoldering pile of broken apple boxes. From a safe distance, I would toss my sacrifice, an effigy of winter as well as hometz, into her flames.

SYLVIA ROTHCHILD, *Family Stories for Every Generation*

Spring represents rebirth, "the rains are over and gone, the blossoms have appeared in the land . . . Arise my darling. My fair one, come away."

SONG OF SONGS 2:11–13

Forgetfulness leads to exile, while memory is the secret of redemption.

BAAL SHEM TOV

Since the Exodus, freedom has always spoken with a Hebrew accent.

HEINRICH HEINE, *Germany from Luther to Kant*

Let all who are hungry, come and eat.
Let all who are in need, come and share the Pesach meal.

from the Passover *Haggadah*

Nor did our mother ever go to the synagogue on Arthur Avenue, except once or twice to hear my brother sing in the choir when she dragged me to join the women's section where the grandmothers held lemonlike fruits to their noses, meant to revive them should the Yom Kippur fast cause them faintness. It was insufferable to know that he earned two dollars for Passover and two dollars for the ten days of Rosh Hashanah-Yom Kippur. I could sing as true and loudly as he and could learn to make the Hebrew sounds as quickly, but they didn't—ever—take girls. It would be gratifying to suggest feminist passion in the resentment, but it dealt only with the stinker amassing two dollars and two dollars more, a fair advance toward a two-wheeler bike, while I earned nothing. Arithmetic, an abomination too, helped feed the angry fires; you could go to the movies twenty times for two dollars, or buy forty big five-cent ice-cream cones. I could be distracted now and then from my brother's pile of gold on Yom Kippur. I liked Yom Kippur; there was something extreme, outrageous, about it, especially when the old men got angry with God. Passover was fun, seders with funny things on the table: baked bones, baked egg, a bitter mash, a sweet mash whose significance we were told and forgot in sipping wine and hunting for the hidden matzo. After we all sang "Chad Gad Yoh," something about a little goat in one of those songs that got bigger and bigger (like "Old MacDonald Had a Farm"), we were dumped on a pile of coats in the bedroom to lie in a nest, like birds, to sleep on warm clouds like Wynken, Blynken, and Nod. Passover meant *bubeluch*, plump matzo meal pancakes covered with sugar, and it meant, on rainy days when we took lunch to school, matzo smeared with chicken fat or, best of all, a cold scrambled egg between two slabs of buttered matzo. And then there was the great classic, *matzo brei*, pieces of matzo soaked in milk, squeezed into a delectable mess, and fried to golden curls and flakes—one of the dishes that evokes piercing darts of nostalgia in every Jewish breast and stories of childhood Passovers complete with lightly drunken uncles.

KATE SIMON, *Bronx Primitive*

The wonderful time, the most joyous time of the year has come . . . The sun is high in the sky . . . the air is free and fresh, soft and clear. On the hill are the first sprouts of spring grass— tender, quivering, green . . . With a screech and a flutter of wings, a straight line of swallows flies overhead, and I am reminded of the Song of Songs. "For lo, the winter is past, the rain is over and gone, the flowers appear on the earth, the time of singing is come."

SHOLOM ALEICHEM

Rabbi Israel Lipkin Salanter was most meticulous in the baking of *Matzos* for Passover. To make certain that everything was done according to the strictest interpretation of Jewish law, he personally undertook to supervise the baking.

One year Rabbi Salanter was bed-ridden and unable to go to the bakery. He instructed two pupils to go in his stead.

As the pupils were about to depart for their assigned task, they asked their teacher:

"Is there anything special which we should watch?"

"Yes," the rabbi replied. "See that the old woman who does the mixing is paid sufficiently. She is a poor widow."
from Philip Goodman, *Rejoice in Thy Festival*

Rosh Hashannah and Yom Kippur are observed in the fall and they celebrate the New Year and repentance for our misdeeds of the past year. The days between these two holidays are called the "Days of Awe," at which time we reflect on our conduct during the previous year and mostly on our relationship with our fellow man. I always liked that Yom Kippur and this period were devoted not so much to our relationship with God as our relationship with humanity. We ask forgiveness from them as we chant the various solemn melodies. The sounding of the shofar is meant to awaken our slumbering souls to the way in which we have conducted our lives during the past year and the manner in which we hope to atone and better ourselves during the year to come.

Although the sounding of the shofar on Rosh Hashana is observed because it is a decree of the Torah, still it has a deep meaning, as if saying: "Wake up from your deep sleep, you who are fast asleep . . . search your deeds and repent; remember your creator . . . examine your souls, mend your ways and deeds. Let everyone give up his evil ways and bad plans."
MAIMONIDES, MISHNEH TORAH: LAWS OF REPENTANCE 3:4

ON THE DAY OF ATONEMENT
Yehudah Amichai

On the day of Atonement in the year 5728, I put on dark holiday clothes and went to the Old City in Jerusalem.

For a long time I stood in the niche of an Arab's shop,
not far from the Nablus Gate, a store
for buttons and zippers and spools of thread
in every shade and snaps and buckles.
A rare light and many colors, like a Holy Ark opened.

I said without speaking that my father
had a store like this for buttons and thread.
I told him without words about the decades,
the causes, events, that now I am here,
and my father's store was burned there and he's buried
    here.

When I finished it was time for the closing prayer.
He too lowered the shutter and locked the door,
and with all those who prayed, I went home.

Until I was twenty-one I had never fasted on the Day of Atonement. I kept only the feasts. But that year—to meet the daughters
of the congregation—I joined a synagogue in our neighborhood.
And since everybody went to synagogue on the Day of Atonement, I thought it would not be nice for me not to go. That
meant, it seemed to me, that I should fast because it would be
hateful to sit, sated and belching among the fasting worshipers.
And it seemed to me that it might even be pleasant in that slight
exaltation that comes from hunger to listen to the cantor and
the choir chanting, to lose myself in the Hebrew of the prayers,
to wrap myself in a silk prayer shawl and in meditation upon
the Eternal forget myself. So I went to synagogue and fasted.

It was a warm day, as warm as a day in summer. About three
o'clock I had gone down and up a depression, I no longer found
the chanting and the prayers tiresome, my collar sticky, the air
close, and, though my head ached a little, my spirit was nimble
and joyous, conversing with the cherubim.

A member of the congregation greeted me. "How are you?" he asked. "You are really fasting?" he added surprised.

"How can you tell?"

"By your lips—they are dry and white. Come, let us go for a walk—a little walk. You will feel better."

"But I feel fine."

"Come, it is lovely outside. We will be back soon."

I was somewhat flattered at his attentions. We walked along the boulevard; the trees had on their holiday leaves of red and yellow. "How is it that a clever young man like you," began my companion, when we were a decent block or so from the synagogue, "carries so little insurance?"

I found my headache worse, excused myself, went home, and ate heartily. Since then I never fast: I am afraid that someone will sell me insurance, or who knows what, when I am weakened.

CHARLES REZNIKOFF, "Meetings and Partings"

Sukkot is in part an old harvest festival, deriving from a time when the Israelites were farmers and would give thanks every autumn when the harvest had been gathered. In fact, it is the prototype of our American festival of Thanksgiving. And in part, it is a commemoration of God's protecting care over Israel during the forty years in the wilderness between Egypt and the Promised Land.

We celebrate Sukkot by building a small annex to our homes, just a few boards and branches, inviting friends in, and drinking wine and eating fruit in it for the week of the holiday. Sukkot is a celebration of the beauty of things that don't last, the little hut which is so vulnerable to wind and rain and will be dismantled at week's end; the ripe fruits which will spoil if not picked and eaten right away; the friends who may not be with us for as long as we would wish; and in northern climates, the beauty of the leaves changing color as they begin the process of dying and falling from the trees. Sukkot comes in the fall. Summer is over and sometimes the evenings are already chilly with the first whispers of winter. It comes to tell us that the world is full of good and beautiful things, food and wine, flowers and sunsets, and autumn landscapes and good company to share them with, but that we have to enjoy them right away because they will not last. They will not wait for us to finish other things and get around to them. It is a time to "eat our bread in gladness and drink our wine with joy" not despite the fact that life does not go on forever but precisely because of that fact.

HAROLD KUSHNER, *When All You've Ever Wanted Isn't Enough*

SUKKOT

Chaim Nachman Bialik

In the *sukkah* nestle darkness and peace,
Through the lattice roof the moonbeams seep;
In its silver cradle on soft fleece
Like a baby the *etrog* lies asleep.

Watching above it, the *lulav* sheaf
Of myrtle and willow leans on the wall,
Weary and silent, and finds relief
Slipping down, asleep in the fall.

Both of them sleep, but their hearts are caught
Each in his dream in his own moonbeam.
Oh, who can fathom the stranger's thought,
Unravel the secret of his dream?

Do they dream of lovely garden ways,
Do their hearts hold fast to homeland skies?
Are they sick of wandering all their days
That have dried their sap and dimmed their eyes?

Or their dream may seal the finished feast,
Since only sorrow unites their lot;
Their bond is torn, their fragrance ceased,
Their beauty marred by spot and rot.

None can tell—through the lattice-shed
Softly the pale, faint moonbeams glide.
In a silver box on its fleecy bed
The *etrog* sleeps by the *lulav*'s side.
The Sukkot Anthology, ed. Phillip Goodman

Night falls. The family dines by candlelight and moonlight in the open air, in the curious hut filled with harvest fragrance. The old holiday melodies and chants sound strangely new outdoors. Maybe it is so cool that they dine in coats. Maybe the weather holds, and they have an idyllic dinner alfresco, in the scented gloom of the *sukkah*. Sometimes it rains, and a half-annoyed half-hilarious scramble indoors ensues. The charm of broken routine, of a new colorful way of doing familiar things, makes Sukkot a seven-day picnic—one that is dedicated and charged with symbol, as well as delightful.
HERMAN WOUK, *This Is My God*

Simchat Torah is celebrated on the last day of Sukkot. It is a joyous holiday marking the end of the weekly reading of the Torah with Deuteronomy and the beginning of another new, yearly cycle with Genesis.

One Simchat Torah evening, the Baal Shem himself danced together with his congregation. He took the scroll of the Torah in his hand and danced with it. Then he laid the scroll aside and danced without it. At this moment, one of his disciples who was intimately acquainted with his gestures, said to his compan-

ions: "Now our master has laid aside the visible, dimensional teachings, and has taken the spiritual teachings unto himself."
MARTIN BUBER, *Tales of the Hasidim*

Hanukkah is firmly documented in history. There are early sources for the story in the first and second books of the Maccabees and in the works of Josephus. It commemorates the successful battle for independence of the Maccabees against the Greeks during a time when the practice of Jewish rituals was outlawed by the Hellenic government. Judah and the Maccabees liberated the temple from defilement by the Greeks and one small cruse of oil miraculously lasted for eight days.

Judah and his brothers and the entire congregation of Israel decreed that the days of the dedication of the altar should be kept with gladness and joy at their due season, year after year, for eight days from the twenty-fifth of the month of Kislev.
1 MACCABEES 4:59

What's the best holiday? Hanukkah of course . . . You eat pancakes every day, spin your dreidel to your heart's content and from all sides money comes pouring in. What holiday can be better than that?
SHOLOM ALEICHEM in Philip Goodman, *Rejoice in Thy Festival*

A Tale of a Candelabrum

A young man once left his father and spent many days in other countries. He lived among strangers.

Somewhat later he returned to his father and boasted that in the foreign lands he had learned a rare craft: how to make a candelabrum with unrivaled skill.

And he requested that his father gather all those whose occupation was the making of candelabra so that he could show them his great wisdom in the craft.

And so the father did.

He brought together all those who occupied themselves with this craft, so that they could see the greatness of his son, what he had accomplished during the days he had spent among strangers.

And when they had all come together the son took out a Menorah he had made.

And it was ugly in the eyes of all the craftsmen.

And the father went to them and begged them to tell him the truth.

So they were compelled to make known the truth, that the Menorah was very ugly. Meanwhile the son kept boasting, "Do you realize the wisdom that lies in my work?"

And his father informed him that it did not seem at all beautiful in the eyes of the others.

Answered the son, "But thereby have I shown my greatness. For I have demonstrated to all of them their defects. For in this candelabrum may be found the defects of each of the craftsmen who abide here.

"You see, don't you, that in the eyes of one this part of the candelabrum is ugly, while another part seems to him very beautiful. With another of the craftsmen it is the opposite: Just the part that seems ugly to his friend is beautiful and wondrous in his eyes. And so it is with all of them. That which is bad in the eyes of one is beautiful in the eyes of his fellow. I made this Menorah solely from defects, in order to show them that each has a defect, that they do not possess perfection. In truth, however, I can make the candelabrum as it should be."

NACHMAN OF BRATSLAV, *A Treasury of Yiddish Stories,*
ed. Irving Howe and Eileen Greenberg

The spirit of Purim is best captured in the Talmudic passage: "It is the obligation of each person to be so drunk [on Purim] as to not be able to tell the difference between 'Blessed be Mordechai' and 'Cursed be Haman.'" (Megillah 7b) *It is a joyful holiday celebrated because the Jews of Persia were saved from annihilation when Queen Esther conveyed to her husband, King Ahasvarus, Haman's terrible plan.*

So many Hamans and but one Purim.
YIDDISH PROVERB

Wearing a silk kerchief and a plain apron—a combination of holiday and weekday attire—Mama stood by the table, practically at her wit's end. It was no trifle, you know, receiving almost a hundred Purim sweet-platters and sending out a like number. Mama had to be careful not to omit anyone or make any mistakes, God forbid; she also had to remember what sort of platter to send to whom. For instance, if someone favored you with a fruit-cut, two jam-filled pastries, a poppy-seed square, two tarts, a honey bun and two sugar cookies, it was customary to give in return two fruit-cuts, one jam-filled pastry, two poppy-seed squares, one tart, two honey buns, and three sugar cookies.

One had to have the brains of a prime minister not to create the sort of first-class muddle which once took place, alas, in our village. What happened was that one certain Rivke-Beyle mistakenly shipped back to one of the rich matrons the very same platter of Purim goodies that the rich matron had sent her. You should have seen the scandal it caused. The squabble that broke out between the husbands blossomed into a full-blown feud—smacks, denunciations and unending strife, as usual.

SHOLOM ALEICHEM, "Purim Sweet-Platters," *Old Country Tales*

FOOD

WHENEVER THE OLD BEIGE Rambler pulled into the driveway—usually knocking over a few shrubs along the way, the mood in our house changed. Martha, our paternal grandmother, had arrived, and she seemed to have her apron on even before she got out of the car. Each of the children was duly embraced and enveloped by her wide, warm body, and then we all stepped aside as she marched into the kitchen. It was less a visit than a culinary takeover, and we loved it. Our mother, a full-time professor of sociology, had no interest in cooking and avoided it whenever possible. My love of food, its secrets and its joys, is the singular legacy of my Grandma Martha.

I learned the alchemy of flour and yeast and sugar. I watched her knead and dice and blend with the ease and confidence of a master. The food was delicious, but the real lesson came long before her sponge cake left the oven: the kitchen was studio, theater, and refuge. It became, as it does in the hands of anyone who understands its potential, a place where joy and art and nourishment meet. I learned to love what I was doing, a love I hope to pass on to my children.

Jewish foods are inextricably linked to our holidays and special times—gefilte fish for the Sabbath, latkes on Hanukkah, blintzes on Shavuoth, hamentaschen on Purim, matzah and macaroons on Passover, with countless variations among the Eastern European and Sephardic traditions. Other gastronomic specialties like chicken soup and bagels have become part of mainstream Americana. Before we knew what was good for us, we knew what we liked. While some nutritional atrocities like gribines and kishka, give new meaning to the term "Jewish guilt," the obsession or love affair between eating and life began long ago.

In the Bible, food is a ubiquitous subject—Abraham goes to great lengths to provide a feast for the three angels. He uses "choice flour" and "a calf, tender and choice," as if following a gourmet cookbook. I still want the recipe for the lentil soup made by Jacob for Esau in exchange for his birthright—it must have been some pot of soup! When the Jews complained in the wilderness that the meals had been much better in Egypt, from which they had just fled, God sent down the Manna. "Now the manna was like coriander seed and its color was like the color of b'dolach [crystal]. The people would stroll and gather it, and grind it in a mill or pound it in mortar and cook it in a pot or make it into cakes, and it tasted like the taste of dough kneaded with oil . . ." (Numbers 11:7–9) It seems that they all had their own recipes, and like all chefs, they fought about the menu.

Claudia Roden, in her beautiful *The Book of Jewish Food* writes, "Every cuisine tells a story. Jewish food tells the story of an uprooted, migrating people and their vanished worlds. It lives in people's minds and has been kept alive because of what it evokes and represents." The dishes we prepare and share celebrate our roots and symbolize continuity. Each time I roll the pastry dough for mandelbrot, I am somehow in the company of Grandma Martha, dipping her hand into the canister for just a bit more flour. The dough doesn't stick but the memory does.

A quotation at the right moment is like bread in a famine.
TALMUD

A wise word is not a substitute for a piece of herring.
SHOLOM ALEICHEM

*In addition to watching Grandma Martha prepare challahs, fish,
soups, and pies for years on the holidays at our home when I was
a child, I spent time in Florida (of course) with her, where at age
sixteen, I learned her secret to creamed herring when she took a
jar of Vita herring, emptied it of its contents, and mixed them
with sour cream and a little sugar—try it!*

The worm in horseradish who thinks he's in heaven is only expressing the worm's capacity for imagination.
FOLK SAYING

*I also found another version by Sholom Aleichem: "The worm in
the radish doesn't think there is anything sweeter."*

Said Israel Baal Shem Tov one day to a simpleton who didn't
understand the value of bagels: "There are many non-Jews in
the wheat field where you work. Take the bagel which you carry
with you and throw it toward them. You will see how they come
to you."

And so it happened that only an hour after the simpleton had
left the famed Hasidic master, he fell into a swiftly flowing river.
The non-Jews were far away at the top of the mountain. How
was he to let them know that he was drowning? Then he remembered that in his pocket was a roll with the power to save
him, its round shape a symbol of life itself. With his last bit of
strength he threw it to the people on the mountain. And, with
the help of the Almighty, just as the Bescht had told him, the
people came to save him from drowning in the river.

Which all goes to show you as one pundit proclaimed several decades ago, a bagel (even a soggy one) is much more than a doughnut with rigor mortis.

PATTI SHOSTECK, A *Lexicon of Jewish Cooking*

This is the original biblical source for challah:

You shall take fine flour and bake it into twelve loaves; each loaf shall be two tenth-ephah. You shall put pure frankincense on each stack and it shall be a remembrance for the bread, a fire-offering for God.

LEVITICUS 24:5–7

I love to bake, but prefer to buy our challah. It's probably been around for years, but my family has only recently discovered a wonderful "pull-apart" challah, divided into twelve sections, available at our local bakery in Manhattan. I highly recommend it, though as with all favorite foods, I suspect every neighborhood has its treasures. For those who truly love to bake their own bread, the following recipe from an old friend is as reliable as they come. In fact, all the recipes here are from relatives and friends.

——

HADASSAH NADICH'S CHALLAH

MAKES 2 LARGE CHALLAHS

3 *cups bread flour*
4 *cups unbleached flour*
3 *large eggs*
½ *cup sugar*
½ *cup oil*
3 *teaspoons salt*
2 *packages dry yeast*

1 egg white mixed with 1 teaspoon water
½ cup sesame seeds (optional)

Dissolve yeast in 2 cups warm water. Let sit 10 minutes. Add sugar, oil, eggs, salt. Gradually mix in flour. Knead for 8 minutes or until elastic.

Put in greased bowl, cover, and let rise until doubled in bulk (about 1 hour). Punch down.

Shape into 2 braids. Let rise 30 minutes. Brush with egg wash and sprinkle with sesame seeds.

Bake at 350 degrees for 30–40 minutes or until brown.

———

My grandmother, of course, made her own bread and taught me to do it at a young age. It never seemed worth the trouble; however, her mandel is another story . . .

———

GRANDMA MARTHA'S MANDEL

MAKES 50 MANDEL

4 large eggs, room temperature
1½–2 cups sugar
¾ cup vegetable oil
1 teaspoon vanilla extract
grated lemon rind
4–4½ cups unbleached all-purpose flour
2 teaspoons baking powder
¼ teaspoon salt
6 ounces chopped walnuts or almonds
Cinnamon and raisins (optional)
(continued)

1. Preheat oven to 350 degrees. Grease 2 cookie sheets.

2. Beat the eggs and sugar in a mixing bowl until light and fluffy. Add the oil, vanilla, and lemon rind and mix thoroughly.

3. Sift the rest of the dry ingredients and add to the sugar mixture. Mix until blended (do not overmix) and add the nuts as the dough starts to come together. Add the cinnamon and raisins.

4. Knead the dough on a floured surface, adding flour if necessary. (Martha used to put the bowl in the refrigerator so it wouldn't be too sticky to handle.) Divide the dough into two or three balls and roll into a log. Place the logs on the prepared cookie sheet.

5. Bake until light golden, about 35 minutes. Let stand for at least 10 minutes outside the oven.

6. Cut the logs diagonally into ½-inch slices and lay them on the cookie sheet and put them back in the oven for 15 minutes or turn the oven off and leave them in for at least 1 hour.

NOTE: They store well in a container for up to 2 weeks and freeze very well.

———

Gefilte fish without chrain is punishment enough.
YIDDISH FOLK SAYING

———

EDITH SILVERSTEIN'S GEFILTE FISH

MAKES 20 TO 22 PIECES

*5 pounds whitefish and pike ground. Save the
heads and bones*
1 cup grated onions
½ cup matzoh meal (optional, helps with forming)

½–¾ cup ice water

2 tablespoons sugar

Salt and pepper to taste

3 large eggs

2 large onions

3 carrots

To the ground fish, add grated onions, matzoh meal, and ice water. Add the sugar, and salt and pepper to taste. Mix well. Add eggs and continue to mix with a chopping motion. The more you mix and chop, the tighter the consistency becomes. The mixture should glisten and be firm enough to form oval balls.

Fill a large pot with water, place head and bones of fish on bottom. Cut up the onions and put them in the pot. Season with salt, pepper, and a drop of sugar.

Bring water to a boil. Form fish mixture into oval-shaped balls the size of your choice and add to boiling water. It will be easier to handle fish if you dip your hands in ice water. After all the fish balls have been added, slice carrots diagonally and add to fish. Cover pot and cook for 2 hours on a low light.

———

Jacob's blessing of his grandchildren: "May they multiply like fish in the midst of the land."

GENESIS 48:16

Meat and fish are Sabbath delights; it's also not bad on other nights.

YIDDISH FOLK SAYING

Purim and *Homentaschen* brought this on.

As I was picking the savory poppy seeds from my teeth, I remembered other flavors and odors that were part of our traditional Jewish past; the taste sensations that were part of Momma's household, and I feel like Pavlov's dog as my mouth recalls:

Matzohs gently coated in chicken fat over which a good healthy *tsibbeleh* had been rubbed. This rubbing the half-onion over the matzoh became in itself an experience in ecstatic anticipation. I've never sampled marijuana but I can't imagine that it would produce a more glowing sensation than golden chicken fat on hemstitched boards . . .

The child was ushered into the world with an array of herring. A *Briss* meant HERRING. For months before the great day our house was inhabited by pickled herrings. Jars, big ones, little ones, glass and clay ones. Eyes, herring eyes, staring at you through windows, in clothing closets, in kitchen closets, on fire escapes—the phosphorescent glow of herrings swinging on onion-hoops. (Notes from a psychiatrist's casebook.)

What better lunch for a school child than cold *koogle* from the previous night with a crust that looked like the scales of a prehistoric mammal, with a side dish of yesterday's *tsimmes* and a seeded roll oozing *hock-flaish* in all directions. For dessert, a penny for a "twist" and back to school raring to go—to sleep. You can imagine the enthusiasm of forty-two such well-oiled scholars for the remainder of the afternoon. What with the noon sun pouring through the windows and the teacher's sweet and gentle voice, the odds were 30 to 1 against arithmetic; and the unceasing parade to the watertrough and other places.

During a holiday, there were special delicacies.

Momma's home-baked *choleh* which was so arranged that you didn't have to slice it. There were bulges all around which you just pulled out of their sockets with ease and *toonked* into nice, oily soup with big eyes that looked up at you from the plate. The sought-after prize in the soup, like the trinket in the cracker-jack box, was a small unhatched egg which Momma had found in the chicken. There was one egg and eight children. What a strain on Momma's impartiality to choose the deserving child. The *ayeleh* usually went to the girls because of some folk-theory about fertility.

Soup could offer a variety of surprises—*kreplach* (meat balls with sports jackets), exquisitely shaped by the sculptural genius of a *balabusteh*, who always planned the structure of the *kreple* so that a tempting bit of the buried treasure should show through, just enough to make the mouth water.

Or soup might contain *lokshen*, which hung like weeping willows over the *flaishegeh leffel*. The excess lokshen could either be sucked into the mouth or bitten into.

What better contribution to *fressen* have we given the world than the incomparable *kishkeh* (sections of fire hose)? They tell me my *zadeh* stuffed his own kishkeh with cow's kishkeh to the age of 94. He carried around a permanent heartburn which kept his body warm and protected him from the severe Russian winters.

SAM LEVENSON in *A Treasury of Jewish Humor*, ed. Nathan Ausubel

A newly-wed couple came before a rabbi with the request that he issue a divorce to them. The rabbi asked them what led them to reach this grave decision after such a short married life.

The husband first presented his grievance:

"I work hard all week. When the Sabbath arrives, I feel I'm entitled to some slight enjoyment. Upon returning home from the morning services in the synagogue, I recite the *Kiddush*. My wife then serves stuffed fish, soup with noodles, chicken and vegetables, and when I cannot eat another morsel she brings out the *Kugel*. I demand that the *Kugel* be served first so that I can really enjoy eating it while I still have an appetite."

The young wife defended her action thus:

"It was a tradition in my father's house—which I feel binding upon me—that the *Kugel* is served at the end of the Sabbath meal. Rabbi, would you want me to violate a Jewish custom?"

The rabbi thoughtfully pondered for a while and then rendered his decision:

"Henceforth, two *Kugels* shall be served: one *Kugel* at the start of the Sabbath meal which will be eaten with appetite, and the second at the end so that a Jewish custom won't be ignored. Now, return home and live in peace."

"The Priority of Kugel" in Philip Goodman, *Rejoice in Thy Festival*

———

EDITH SILVERSTEIN'S STOVETOP POTATO KUGEL

SERVES 8

Grate 3 large potatoes. Add 2 eggs, salt and pepper to taste. Soak 2 rolls or old challah in cold water. Squeeze out very well. Add to mixture and blend in well.

Pour oil into an 8- or 9-inch fry pan. Oil should be about ¼ inch deep. Put pan on medium fire until oil is very hot.

Pour mixture into fry pan and keep a medium-high flame until mixture begins to brown on bottom and hold its shape. Turn flame to very low for ½ hour.

Turn out kugel onto plate and slip back into pan with bottom side up. Continue on low flame until the top which is now on the bottom browns and gets crisp.

Before serving, drain on paper towel. At this point the kugel can be heated in the oven until ready to serve.

———

I find garlic a joy—an extraordinarily versatile ingredient in countless dishes. For me, the Italians use it better than anyone else, but no doubt there are some Sephardic Jews who would differ.

In Roman times, Marcus Aurelius criticized Jews for exuding its smell. Historians suggest that its purported power as an aphrodisiac was the overriding reason for its popularity in foods. Rabbi Ezra said it should be eaten specifically on Friday nights because "it promotes love and arouses desire."

Five things were said of garlic:
It satisfies your hunger.
It keeps the body warm.
It makes your face bright.
It increases a man's potency.
And it kills parasites in the bowels.
Some people say that it also encourages love and removes jealousy.
TALMUD: BAVA KAMMA 82a

MY TUSCAN CHICKEN WITH GARLIC

SERVES 8

2 chickens, cut into fourths or eighths
1 bottle dry white wine
A few sprigs sage, rosemary, and thyme
2 ounces dried porcini mushrooms
1 14-ounce can whole tomatoes, chopped, or 5 medium seeded tomatoes, chopped
At least 4 cloves garlic
Salt and pepper

Place chicken, herbs, and garlic in a large pot with about ¾ bottle of wine to cover (I usually use a bottle of wine for about 2 to 3 chickens). Marinate for at least one hour. Cover the mushrooms in the rest of the wine in a separate bowl.

Turn on stove to a very high light and reduce the wine until there's almost none and so that chicken is browned. Add mushrooms, tomatoes, salt, and pepper. Place, covered, in oven at 325°–350°F for 1 hour.

―――――

To claim that a bagel has five hundred calories, smacks, to me, of anti-Semitism.

JUDY GRAUBART

Dating back at least to Talmudic times, cholent was the traditional stew for the Sabbath midday meal and the only hot dish of the day. It is prepared on Friday afternoon and left in the oven overnight. There are so many different versions of cholent in Eastern and Western tradition that rather than listing the hundreds of possible ingredients I decided to include a simple, delicious recipe from my sister-in-law Sheira.

―――――

SHEIRA'S CHOLENT

SERVES 12

Layer in a large casserole:

2 onions, chopped irregularly

½ bag each: dried barley, red kidney beans, white lima beans, and northern, navy, or cranberry beans on top of the onions

6 potatoes, quartered, on top of the beans

2–3 pounds flanken or deckel on top of the potatoes

Potato kugel, kishka or kneidlach may be added as a final layer

Fill with water to top and season with salt, pepper, garlic, and ketchup or barbecue sauce (almost ½ bottle)

Place in oven at 225 degrees overnight—"no basting or peeping."

———

Good flour should be white with a faint yellow tinge; if wet and kneaded, it should work dry and elastic; if a lump of dry flour is thrown against the wall it should adhere altogether and not fall apart; good flour when squeezed in the hand should retain the shape thus given.

American Jewess, 1895

May you eat chopped liver with onions, shmaltz herring, chicken soup with dumplings, baked carp with horseradish, braised meat with vegetable stew, latkes, tea with lemon, every-day—and may you choke on every mouthful.

YIDDISH CURSE

May he grow like an onion: with his head in the ground and his feet in the air!

YIDDISH CURSE

It doesn't pay to look too closely into a cholent or into a bridal match.

YIDDISH FOLK SAYING

My mother used to buy one pound of meat and make three pounds of hamburgers. You know how? We had a slogan in our house. It said, "old rolls never die." Everything went into a hamburger. After a while, my mother learned to make chopped meat completely without meat and I liked it that way.

SAM LEVENSON in Darryl Lyman, *Jewish Comedy Catalog*

A woman who eats meat and drinks wine [during her pregnancy] will have healthy children. One who eats eggs will have children with large eyes. One who eats fish will have charming children.

One who eats parsley will have exceptionally handsome children. One who eats coriander will have fleshy children. One who eats etrog [the lemonlike yellow fruit used on Sukkot] will have fragrant children.

King Shapur's daughter, whose mother had eaten etrog [while pregnant with her], used to be lifted in front of her father to provide his favorite perfume.

CHAIM NACHMAN BIALIK and YEHOSHUA HANA RAVNITZKY,
Book of Legends

The greatest kosher pickles in the world, I remember, were sold by an elderly woman forty years ago. She stood in a store on the corner of Clinton and Rivington Streets completely surrounded by barrels. She sold very sour pickles, pickled tomatoes, red peppers. Her real delicacy was sauerkraut. It cost a penny and she plowed into the barrel and brought out a fistful which she dropped on a piece of brown paper. I mentioned the store to an old-timer who told me that the woman had educated her three sons with her scanty profits. She was there in every sort of weather — rain, cold, or blazing heat wave. No one, to my knowledge, has ever duplicated her sauerkraut.

HARRY GOLDEN, *You're Entitle'*

One by one, as their cups of tea were filled, the hungry workers dispersed into groups. Seated on window sills, table-tops, machines, and bales of shirts, they munched black bread and herring and sipped tea from saucers. And over all rioted the acrid odor of garlic and onions . . . If I lived in America for a hundred years I couldn't get used to the American eating. What can make the mouth so water like the taste and the smell from herring and onions?

ANZIA YEZIERSKA, *Hungry Hearts*

I list *blintz* and *blintzes* together, because I never heard of any-
body eating only one.

LEO ROSTEN, *The Joys of Yiddish*

My family has celebrated the Shavuoth holiday for the last ten
years in the warm, comfortable home of my brother's in-laws in
Atlantic Beach. We all usually return home five pounds heavier—
these heavenly blintzes account for some of the weight gain.

———

EDITH SILVERSTEIN'S BLINTZES

MAKES 12–15

Pancakes

3 large eggs

½ teaspoon salt

1½ cups water

⅔ cup flour or cake meal on Passover

Combine eggs, salt, and water. Add gradually to flour or cake
meal stirring constantly to avoid lumps.

Brush the bottom and sides of a 6-inch fry pan lightly with oil.
When pan becomes hot, lift pan off heat, add a generous tablespoon of batter, and tilt the pan in a circular motion to spread
batter evenly and thinly over the bottom of the pan. If you have
too much batter in the pan after the bottom is covered, pour the
excess batter back into the bowl. Return the pan to medium heat
and cool until set and edges fall away from pan. Use fork to lift
slightly. Turn out on wax paper. Repeat until all batter is
used up.

(continued)

Filling

1 pound farmer cheese

2 eggs

⅓ cup sugar, or to taste

¼ teaspoon cinnamon

Pinch of salt

Mix all the ingredients until very smooth. Place a heaping tablespoon of filling in center of each pancake. Fold in sides and roll up securely.

Freeze blintzes. When ready to use, fry frozen blintzes until brown on both sides.

———

Schizophrenia is better than eating alone.

OSCAR LEVANT

Our greatest delight in all seasons was "delicatessen"—hot spiced corned beef, pastrami, rolled beef, hard salami, soft salami, chicken salami, bologna, frankfurter specials and the thinner, wrinkled hot dogs always taken with mustard and relish and sauerkraut, and whenever possible, to make the treat fully real, with potato salad, baked beans, and french fries which had been bubbling in the black wire fryer deep in the iron pot. At Saturday twilight, as soon as the delicatessen store reopened after the Sabbath rest, we reached into it panting for the hot dogs sizzling on the gas plate just inside the window. The look of that blackened empty gas plate had driven us wild all through the wearisome Sabbath day. And now, as the electric sign blazed up again, lighting up the words JEWISH NATIONAL DELICATESSEN, it was as if we had entered our rightful heritage.

ALFRED KAZIN, *A Walker in the City*

Whoever was burned on hot farfel will blow at cold farfel.
YIDDISH FOLK SAYING

SCENE: A *restaurant.*
FIRST CUSTOMER: "Give me the *borsht.*"
WAITER: "Take my advice: have the chicken soup."
SECOND CUSTOMER: "I'll have pea soup."
WAITER: "Don't take the pea soup—take the barley."

The soup is brought, the customers served.

FIRST CUSTOMER: "This chicken soup is marvelous! The best I ever tasted!"
SECOND CUSTOMER: "Waiter! Why didn't you recommend me the chicken soup?"
WAITER: "You didn't ask for the *borsht!*"
LEO ROSTEN, *The Joys of Yiddish*

Even if the kugel doesn't quite work out, you still have the noodles.
SHOLOM ALEICHEM

Beauty diffuses itself in the world as an apple.
ZOHAR

HEALTH

*I*F YOUR MEDIA DIET consists of magazines and talk shows, it's easy to assume that "healthy living" started around the time of oat bran and designer sneakers. But the truth is that medicine, psychiatry, and nutrition are only just beginning to catch up with conclusions that predate Maimonides.

The ancient Romans extolled "a sound mind in a sound body." The Greeks created the gymnasium as a site for conversation as much as for exercise and bathing, although I wonder how the scholars and peddlers had time to go to the gym. Keeping the body clean and healthy, along with proper eating habits, is considered a religious duty. We honor God by maintaining our good health. The body, lent to us for a lifetime, is, after all, the home of the soul.

Once when the sage Hillel had finished a lesson with his pupils, he accompanied them for a while on their way home.

"Master," they asked, "where are you going?"

"To perform a religious duty," he answered.

"What duty is that?"

"To bathe in the bathhouse."

"Is that a religious duty?" they asked.

"If somebody is appointed to scrape and clean the statues of the king that stand in the theaters and circuses, is paid for the work, and even associates with nobility," he answered, "how much more should I, who am created in the image and likeness of God, take care of my body!" (Leviticus Rabbah 34:3)

The preservation of human life takes precedence over all the commandments. The Torah gave specific consent for human healing in the phrase "and heal he shall heal." (Exodus 21:19) The Talmud states, "He who has saved one life is as if he saved a whole world." (Sanhedrin 37a) From these passages, we learn that a patient has a religious obligation to seek the help of a physician, thus the birth of the Jewish doctor.

Maimonides wrote numerous medical books and served as personal physician to the family of Sultan Saladin of Egypt. He investigated matters of health, nutrition, and medicine as seriously as the complex laws of religious ritual. Nearly seven centuries before the newspapers and *60 Minutes* spoke glowingly of red wine, Maimonides wrote about its benefits.

While contemporary science continues to debate the intricacies of endorphins and receptors and Prozac, the mind/body connection is already a foregone fact to those who have discovered the power of exercise. I always enjoyed sports, but I discovered running after I met my husband. It began as a challenge, grew to an addiction, and has remained (with six NYC marathons behind me and assorted stress fractures to prove it) solace and antidote. I can enter Central Park in the foulest of moods and exit smiling. Even blessed with good health, we can feel overwhelmed with responsibility and anxiety. Exercise shifts that equation, as accomplishment and activity alleviate stress, and the mind works again. But don't take my word for it . . .

The body is the soul's house. Shouldn't we therefore take care of our house so that it doesn't fall into ruin?
PHILO, *The Worse Attacks the Better*

Eat a third and drink a third and leave the remaining third of your stomach empty.

Then, when you get angry, there will be sufficient room for your rage.
TALMUD, GITTEN 70a

The sages said in the name of Rav: It is forbidden to live in a city that has no bathhouse.
TALMUD: KIDDUSHIN 4:12

Respect your own body as the receptacle, messenger and instrument of the spirit.
S. R. HIRSCH, *The Nineteen Letters, no. 11*

If you marvel at the waters of the sea, that the sweet and the salty do not mingle, think of the tiny human head, where the fluids of its many fountains do not mingle.
NUMBERS RABBAH 18:22

The following excerpt from Maimonides could easily be incorporated into any contemporary book on healthy living.

One does not consider exercise though it is the main principle in keeping one's health and in the repulsion of most illnesses . . .

And there is no such thing as excessive body movements and exercise. Because body movements and exercise will ignite natural heat and superfluities will be formed in the body, but they will be expelled. However, when the body is at rest, the natural heat is suppressed and the superfluities remain . . .

Exercise removes the harm caused by most bad habits, which

most people have. And no movement is as beneficial, according to the physicians, as body movements and exercise.

Exercise refers both to strong and weak movements, provided it is a movement that is vigorous and affects breathing, increasing it. Violent exercise causes fatigue, and not everyone can stand fatigue or needs it. It is good for the preservation of health to shorten the exercises.

MAIMONIDES, *The Preservation of Youth*

Three things restore a person's good spirits: beautiful sounds, sights, and smells.

TALMUD: BERAKHOT 57b

Your health comes first—you can always hang yourself later.

FOLK SAYING

Emotional experiences cause marked changes in the body which are clear and visible to all and bear witness in clear testimony.

You see a man strongly built whose voice is powerful and pleasant and whose countenance is splendid. When he is affected all of a sudden by a feeling of great disgust, his facial expression falls and loses its luster. The light of his countenance changes, his posture becomes low and his voice hoarse and weak . . .

You see quite the reverse in a man whose body is weak, whose appearance is strange and whose voice is low. When something happens to him which causes him to rejoice greatly, you will see how his body becomes strong, his voice rises, his face brightens, his movements become manifest in his face and eyelids . . .

. . . When one is overpowered by imagination, prolonged meditation and avoidance of social contact, which he never exhibited before, or when one avoids pleasant experiences which

were in him before, the physician should do nothing before he improves the soul by removing the extreme emotions.
MAIMONIDES, *The Preservation of Youth*

A man of good upbringing is content with little, and he is not short of breath when he goes to bed.

The moderate eater enjoys healthy sleep; he rises early, feeling refreshed.

But sleeplessness, indigestion, and colic are the lot of the glutton.
Wisdom of Ben Sira

As far as possible the meat [eaten] should be that of hens or roosters and their broth should also be taken, because this sort of fowl has virtue in rectifying corrupted humors, whatever the corruption may be, and especially the black humors, so much so that the physicians have mentioned that chicken broth is beneficial in leprosy.
MAIMONIDES, *Treatise on Accidents*

In order to strengthen the vital powers, one should employ musical instruments and tell patients gay stories which will make the heart swell and narratives that will distract the mind and cause them and their friends to laugh.
MAIMONIDES, *The Preservation of Youth*

I have been eating bread with jam in the morning for years and I stand by the Talmud on this one:

Thirteen things were said concerning eating bread in the morning:

It protects against heat and cold, winds and demons.

It makes the simple wise, causes a person to win lawsuits, and helps a person to study and teach Torah, to have his words heeded, and to retain scholarship.

A person who eats in the morning doesn't exhale a bad odor and lives with his wife without lusting after other women.

Morning bread also kills the worms in a person's intestines.

And some people say it gets rid of jealousy and encourages love . . .

A proverb says: "Sixty runners speed along but cannot overtake the person who breaks bread in the morning."

TALMUD: BAVA MEZIA 107b

Since by keeping the body in health and vigor one walks in the ways of God—it being impossible during sickness to have any understanding or knowledge of the Creator—it is a man's duty to avoid whatever is injurious to the body and cultivate habits conducive to health and vigor.

MAIMONIDES, MISHNEH TORAH: LAWS CONCERNING MORAL DISPOSITIONS AND ETHICAL CONDUCT

The purpose of maintaining the body in good health is to [make it possible for you to] acquire wisdom.

MAIMONIDES, MISHNEH TORAH

You may be free from sin, but if your body is not strong, your soul will be too weak to serve God aright. Maintain your health and preserve your strength.

BAAL SHEM TOV, The Hasidic Anthology

The benefits of wine are many if it is taken in the proper amount, as it keeps the body in a healthy condition and cures many illnesses.

But the knowledge of its consumption is hidden from the masses. What they want is to get drunk, and inebriety causes harm . . .

The small amount that is useful must be taken after the food leaves the stomach. Young children should not come close to it because it hurts them and causes harm to their body and soul . . .

The older a man is, the more beneficial the wine is for him. Old people need it most.

MAIMONIDES, *The Preservation of Youth*

Analysis makes for unity, but not necessarily for goodness.

SIGMUND FREUD

The body often seems to have more insight than the soul, and man thinks frequently far better with his back and belly than with his head.

HEINRICH HEINE, "Romantic School"

A person should not eat meat unless he has a special appetite for it.

TALMUD: HULLIN 842

There are eight things that taken in large quantities are bad but in small quantities are helpful:

Travel, sex, wealth, work, wine, sleep, hot baths, and bloodletting.

TALMUD: GITTIN 70a

Well, you do not have to agree with everything in this book or the Talmud. I am really going to have to go with another school of thought on the travel and sex and as for bloodletting, well . . .

Do not sit too much, for sitting aggravates hemorrhoids;
Do not stand too much, for standing hurts the heart;
Do not walk too much, for walking hurts the eyes.

So, spend one third of your time sitting, one third standing, and one third walking.

TALMUD: KETUBBOT 111a

Washing your hands and feet in warm water every evening is better than all the medicines in the world.

TALMUD: SHABBAT

If a Jew breaks a leg, he says, "Praised be God that I did not break both legs." If he breaks both legs, he says, "Praised be God that I did not break my neck."

YIDDISH FOLK SAYING

Running has been my joy for nearly twenty years. I could not possibly prepare a section on health without quoting one of my heroes.

I have been asked everywhere I go: Why do people run the marathon? Sure, there is a sense of status we gain among our peers. But I think the real reasons are more personal. I think it is because we need to test our physical, emotional, or creative abilities. After all, in practical life we cannot "give it our all." We can't grow wings and fly. We can't sing without a great voice, or dance when we aren't dancers. Most of us won't perform on a stage. But whether a person is a world-class athlete or a four-hour runner, the marathon gives us a stage. In this case, it's the road, where we can perform and be proud . . .

In an unequal world, in this one endeavor people of vastly differing abilities share something in common: the act of going the distance. Whether it's two hours or four or five, the effort and achievement are similar.

FRED LEBOW, *The New York Road Runners Club Complete Guide to Running*

When I started running, I had the idea I had to be very good to participate. I remember how embarrassed I was the first time I called to inquire about a race and had to tell the official I was 38 years old. One of my first races was a five-miler near Yankee Stadium. People who raced were fairly serious in those days. There were only 60 people, and I came in 59th, beating a 70 year old. But I was pleased I was able to finish without walking.
FRED LEBOW, *The New York Road Runners Club Complete Guide to Running*

The Jewish doctor of my insurance agency lives down the block from my house. He has just opened an office and is waiting for customers. He constantly complains that *he* is sick. When a patient drops in once in a blue moon, he takes him into the *vaytik room* (that's what Jewish patients call the waiting room) where there are numerous shelves filled with (borrowed) surgical instruments which he doesn't begin to know how to use. He lights up the electric machines with the red and green bulbs and the deafening clatter, and says, in a professorial-solemn voice: "Your stomach has to be . . . [he doesn't say what] but don't be afraid. You'll come in twice a week regularly, and we may not have to use those instruments." He points to the huge glass shelves stacked with the nickel-plated paraphernalia.

The doctor's back pockets bulge with bottles of urine, which he is constantly pulling out together with his filthy handkerchief. He is always telling my applicants that their "water" is no good.
MOSHE NADIR in *How We Lived* ed. Irving Howe and Kenneth Libo

I went to a psychoanalyst who wanted to know about my childhood, when I could barely remember whether I took a taxi or a bus to his office that day.
Arthur in PADDY CHAYEFSKY, *The Tenth Man*

When you need a physician esteem him a god;
When he has brought you out of danger, you consider him a
  king.
When you have been cured, he becomes human like yourself;
When he sends you the bill, you think him a devil.

JEDADIAH BEN ABRAHAM BEDERSI

The physician should have both technical knowledge and skill
as well as understand the patient's personality and lifestyle.

MAIMONIDES, *The Preservation of Youth*

A Stampede of MDs

A few nights ago I woke up about midnight to a stomach-ache
unknown so far in the annals of human suffering. With what
strength was left in me I crawled to the phone and rang up Dr.
Wasservogel who lives in the flat exactly over ours. Mrs. Wasservogel lifted the receiver and after I had told her that I was
going to pieces with pain, informed me that her husband was
not at home. She advised me to wait half an hour and if the
pain did not cease, call Dr. Blaumilch. I waited a century-long
half hour and before the eyes of my mind there passed my sad
childhood, my years of productive work in a forced labour camp
and my journalistic decline. Then I phoned Dr. Blaumilch, and
his wife replied that her husband did not receive patients on odd
days, I should contact Dr. Greenbutter. I rang up that doctor,
and Mrs. Greenbutter lifted the receiver and laid it to rest at the
foot of the telephone.

For a while I crawled up and down the walls, then I prepared
my last will and testament and left a legacy of $250 for the build-
ing of an auditorium in my name. On the very verge of collapse
I remembered that Yossi, the neighbor's son, was an enthusiastic
radio ham. To cut a long story short: Yossi contacted Lydda

Airport by shortwave radio, and an El Al plane took off carrying with it an S.O.S. message for Cyprus. There, the plane was met by the special courier of the Israel Consulate who dashed off by motorcycle to Luxembourg and from there sent a 500-word cable to Winston Churchill. The British elder Statesman put his personal railway train at the disposal of the Kol Yisrael correspondent who flew to Copenhagen and from there broadcast a dramatic appeal to world public opinion. Canadian Jewry immediately dispatched an ambulance to Holland. The police chief of Rotterdam drove the ambulance all over Europe and collected 37 famous professors and surgeons who arrived here in a jet bomber of the U.S. Air Force.

On the way to Tel Aviv, the convoy was swelled by the participants of the Natanya medical convention, and thus a total of 108 doctors reached my place at dawn. Dr. Wasservogel was awakened by the clatter and din of the buses pulling up, and came running down the steps. I took advantage of his presence and asked him what to do against stomach-ache. He told me I should be more careful of what I eat.

Thus my life was saved by international solidarity. But next time I'll call Queen Elizabeth directly. I can't waste so much time.

EPHRAIM KISHON, *Noah's Ark, Tourist Class*

To a doctor you musn't wish a good year.
YIDDISH FOLK SAYING

How those doctors could ever make a diagnosis on the basis of the symptoms provided by their patients only proves what remarkable practitioners they were:

"How do you feel?"
"How should I feel?"
"What hurts you?"

"What doesn't hurt me?"
"When do you feel badly?"
"When don't I feel badly?"
"When did it start?"
"When will it end better?"
SAM LEVENSON, *You Don't Have to Be in Who's Who to Know
What's What*

Just do me one favor, doctor. Listen to me until I finish. I don't
mean listen to my heart or anything like that. About my sickness,
we'll talk later. In fact, I myself will tell you what's wrong with
me. I just want you to listen to what I have to say, for not every
doctor likes to listen to his patient. Not every doctor lets his
patient talk. That's a bad habit of theirs — they don't let their
patients open their mouths. All they know is how to write pre-
scriptions, look at their watches and take your pulse, your temperature, and your money. But I've been told you're not that sort
of doctor. They say you're still young and you're not as passionate
for the ruble as the rest of them. That's why I came to consult
you about my stomach and get your advice. Look at me now
and you're looking at a man with a stomach. Medical science
says that *everyone* must have a stomach. But when? On condition
that the stomach is a stomach. But when your stomach just isn't
a stomach, your life's not worth a damn. I know what you'll say
next: man must keep living! But I don't need your help for that.
That got me the taste of the strap when I was a boy in Hebrew
school.

My point is that so long as a man lives, he doesn't want to
die. To tell you the truth, I'm not afraid of death at all. First of
all, I'm over sixty. And second of all, I'm the sort of fellow to
whom life and death are the same. That is, sure, living is better
than dying; for who wants to die? Especially a Jew? Especially a
father of eleven children, may they live and be well, and a
wife — despite the fact that she's my third — but a wife for all that.

To make a long story short, I come from Kamenitz, that is, not really from Kamenitz proper, but from a little place not far from Kamenitz . . .

SHOLOM ALEICHEM, "At the Doctor's," *Stories and Satires by Sholom Aleichem*

If a physician cannot give a patient medicine for the body, he should somehow find and give medicine for the patient's soul.

ZOHAR

NATURE

CONCERN FOR THE NATURAL world and compassion for all its creatures began centuries before Greenpeace and PETA. There are numerous passages in the Bible, as well as Talmudic rulings, that deal with the way we interact with nature and the appreciation we must have for all living things. There are ancient texts that deal explicitly with environmental pollution, wasteful destruction, and cruelty to animals. Protection of the bountiful and beautiful earth was not merely a matter of primitive survival — then as now, it offered a glimpse of God's majesty. That reverence and awe lies deep in so much of our literature and poetry. It is one of the oldest messages in history: an homage and a warning that resound through the ages. And it is one that has yet to be learned.

Each person has a favorite retreat — a place where one breathes and thinks differently and sees the world afresh. I have stood alone on a deserted Atlantic beach at the shank of a summer evening with the cold sand under my feet and everything open and vast: the power of the ocean, the clamor of the water and the birds . . . and that light. When I am overcome by the mundane, this is the image I try to recall; it restores my perspective. Even here in Manhattan, in the heart of bedlam, there is the man-made miracle called Central Park—over 840 acres of prime real estate, a cathedral of fields, woods, and trails. What is that magic we all experience when we are in a natural setting? Can we ever appreciate its full effect on us and how badly we need it?

In *Teaching Your Children About God*, Rabbi David Wolpe tells a wonderful Hasidic story about the child of a rabbi who used to wander in the woods. At first his father let him wander, but over time he became concerned. The woods were dangerous. The father did not know what lurked there.

He decided to discuss the matter with his child. One day he took him aside and said, "You know, I have noticed that each day you walk into the woods. I wonder, why do you go there?"

The boy said to his father, "I go there to find God."

"That is a very good thing," the father replied gently. "I am glad you are searching for God. But, my child, don't you know that God is the same everywhere?"

"Yes," the boy answered, "but I'm not."

When God created Adam, he led him around the Garden of Eden and said to him: "Behold my works! See how beautiful they are, how excellent! All that I have created, for your sake did I create it. See to it that you do not spoil and destroy my world: for if you do there will be no one to repair it after you."
ECCLESIASTES RABBAH 7:13

The quality of urban air compared to the air in the deserts and forests is like thick and turbulent water compared to pure and light water. And this is because in the cities with their tall buildings and narrow roads, the pollution that comes from their residents, their wastes and cadavers . . .
MAIMONIDES, *The Preservation of Youth*

Be open-eyed to the great wonders of nature, familiar though they be. But men are more wont to be astonished at the sun's eclipse than at its unfailing rise.

HAYYIM LUZZATTO, *Orhot Tzaddikim*

God established the earth on its foundations,
    so that it shall never totter.
You made the deep cover it as a garment;
    the waters stood above the mountains . . .
Mountains rising, valleys sinking—
    to the place You established for them . . .
You make springs gush forth torrents;
    they make their way between the hills,
Giving drink to all the wild beasts;
    the wild asses slake their thirst.
The birds of the sky dwell beside them
    and sing among the foliage . . .
You make the grass grow for the cattle,
    and herbage for human labor
    that we may get food out of the earth—
Wine that cheers human hearts
    oil that makes the face shine,
    and bread that sustains our life.

PSALM 104:5–15

In his final years, the renowned Rabbi Samson Raphael Hirsch suddenly announced to his students that he was going to Switzerland to climb in the Alps.

"Why?" asked his astonished students.

"Because when I come face to face with the creator of the universe," mused Hirsch, "I know He will look down at me and say 'So, Shimshon, did you see My Alps?' "

Appreciating beauty is an act of devotion. That is why Judaism contains blessings for seeing beautiful mountains, the ocean, a rainbow and other natural sights.

The Talmud advises that one should pray only in a room with windows. To sing to God and not see God's world is a contradiction. The word *chupah* in the marriage ceremony once referred to the traditional covering of the bride and groom — chupat Shamayim — the canopy of the heavens, what the poet Houseman called the "star pavilioned sky."

In the Bible, humanity begins in a garden. Judaism continues using natural metaphors: the Torah is likened to a tree, the Talmud to a sea, the human spirit to the wind. When we move through the world, feel its rhythms, are awestruck by its majesty, absorb its beauty, we are doing more than paying homage to the forces of nature — we are offering a deep, authentic prayer to God.

RABBI DAVID WOLPE, *Jewish Week*

EARTH'S EMBROIDERY
Solomon ibn Gabriol

With the ink of its showers and rains,
with the quill of its lightning, with the
hand of its clouds, winter wrote a letter
upon the garden, in purple and blue.
No artist could ever conceive the like of
that. And this is why the earth, grown
jealous of the sky, embroidered stars in
the folds of the flower-beds.

Even in times of war, it was forbidden to wantonly destroy the enemy's natural resources:

When you besiege a city . . . you shall not destroy its [fruit] trees; if you eat of them, do not cut them down; for man's life depends on the trees of the field.

DEUTERONOMY 20:19

One should be trained not to be destructive. When you bury a person, do not waste garments by burying them in the grave. It is better to give them to the poor than to cast them to worms and moths. Anyone who buries the dead in an expensive garment violates the negative command of *bal tashkit.*

MAIMONIDES, MISHNEH TORAH: LAWS OF MOURNING 14:24

The Souls of Trees

Reb Nachman was once traveling with his Hasidim by carriage, and as it grew dark they came to an inn, where they spent the night. During the night Reb Nachman began to cry out loudly in his sleep, waking up everyone in the inn, all of whom came running to see what had happened.

When he awoke, the first thing Reb Nachman did was to take out a book he had brought with him. Then he closed his eyes and opened the book and pointed to a passage. And there it was written "Cutting down a tree before its time is like killing a soul."

Then Reb Nachman asked the innkeeper if the walls of that inn had been built out of saplings cut down before their time. The innkeeper admitted that this was true, but how did the rabbi know?

And Reb Nachman said: "All night I dreamed I was surrounded by the bodies of those who had been murdered. I was very frightened. Now I know that it was the souls of the trees that cried out to me."

from *Gabriel's Palace,* ed. Howard Schwartz

I can contemplate a tree.

I can accept it as a picture: a rigid pillar in a flood of light, or splashes of green traversed by the gentleness of the blue silver ground.

I can feel it as a movement: the flowing veins around the sturdy, striving core, the sucking of the roots, the breathing of the leaves, the infinite commerce with earth and air, and the growing itself in its darkness.

I can overcome its uniqueness and form so rigorously that I can recognize it only as an expression of the law—those laws according to which a constant opposition of forces is continually adjusted, or those laws according to which the elements mix and separate.

I can dissolve it into a number, into a pure relation between numbers, and eternalize it.

Throughout all of this the tree remains my object and has its place and its time span, its kind and condition.

But it can also happen, if will and grace are joined, that as I contemplate the tree I am drawn into a relation, and the tree ceases to be an It. The power of exclusiveness has seized me.

This does not require me to forgo any of the modes of contemplation. There is nothing that I must not see in order to see, and there is no knowledge that I must forget. Rather, is everything, picture and movement, species and instance, law and number included and inseparably fused.

Whatever belongs to the tree is included: its form and its mechanics, its colors and its chemistry, its conversation with the elements and its conversation with the stars.

MARTIN BUBER, *I and Thou*

Should the emancipation and secularization of the modern age which began with a turning-away, not necessarily from God, but from a god who was the father of men in heaven, end with even more repudiation of an earth who was the Mother of all living creatures under the sky?

HANNAH ARENDT, *The Human Condition*

Rav Huna said, "Any city where there are no green vegetables— a sage may not dwell therein."

TALMUD: ERUVIN 55b

To chop down a fruit-bearing tree is like unto murder.

NACHMAN OF BRATSLAV

I will plant cedars in the wilderness
and acacias, and myrtles and oleasters;
I will set cypresses in the desert
Box trees and elms as well—
That people may see and know,
Consider and comprehend
That God's hand has done this,
That the Holy One of Israel has wrought it!

ISAIAH 41:19

Pray only in a room with windows [to remember the world outside].

TALMUD: BERAKOTH 34b

Meditation and prayer before God are particularly efficacious in grassy fields and amid the trees, since a man's soul is thereby strengthened, as if every blade of grass and every plant united with him in prayer.

NACHMAN OF BRATSLAV

If you should find yourself holding on to a sapling and they tell you that the Messiah has just arrived, first finish planting the tree and then go out and meet the Messiah.

AVOT DE RABBI NATHAN

Whether it is because the faith which creates has ceased to exist in me, or because reality takes shape in the memory alone, the flowers that people show me nowadays for the first time never seem to me to be true flowers.

MARCEL PROUST, *Swann's Way*

Nature uses only the longest threads to weave her patterns, so each small piece of her fabric reveals the organization of the entire tapestry.

RICHARD FEYNMAN

There are three aspects of nature that command our attention: its power, its beauty, and its grandeur. Accordingly, there are three ways in which we may relate to the world—we may exploit it, we may enjoy it, we may accept it in awe. Our age is one in which usefulness is thought to be the chief merit of nature; human beings have indeed become primarily tool-making animals.

There is thus only one way to wisdom: awe. Forfeit your sense of awe, let your conceit diminish your ability to revere, and the universe becomes a market place for you. The loss of awe is the great block to insight. A return to reverence is the first prerequisite for a revival of wisdom, for the discovery of the world as an allusion to God. Wisdom comes from awe rather than from shrewdness. It is evoked not in moments of calculation but in moments of being in rapport with the mystery of reality. The greatest insights happen to us in moments of awe.

ABRAHAM HESCHEL, *God in Search of Man*

Vegetarianism was a way of life for all mankind and animals before the flood in Noah's time. Even when we became meat eaters, the laws relating to butchery were established with concern for the animals.

See, I give you every seed-bearing plant upon all the earth, and every tree that has seed-bearing fruit; they shall be yours for food.
GENESIS 1:29

It is prohibited to kill an animal and its young . . . in such a manner that the young is slain in the sight of its mother, for the pain of the animals under such circumstances is very great. There is no difference in this case between the pain of man and pain of other living beings, since the love and tenderness of the mother for her young ones . . . exist not only in man but in most living beings.
MAIMONIDES, *Guide of the Perplexed* 3:48

People are vegetarians because they say they don't like meat or because they say it is unhealthy. I always liked meat and I think it is perfectly healthy. But I feel animals are not made to be killed. I have my two birds, they are such lovely creatures — the thought of someone eating them makes me sick. I realize that in this world things are made so animals and people have to kill each other. It can't be helped. But it is not my duty to help in this destruction. No human being has what animals have. They should be our teachers and masters, not our food. They are humble, they have humility, they are sincere. They are not something to eat, they are God's beautiful creation.
ISAAC BASHEVIS SINGER, *Conversations*

The attitude toward vegetarianism . . . the attitude toward living creatures is . . . the clearest test of our attitude towards life and towards the world as it really is . . . The ethical regard toward

living creatures that involves no hope of reward, no utilitarian motives—secret or open, such as honor—shows us . . . the significance of righteousness and all the other desired traits . . .
A. D. GORDON in *Judaism and Vegetarianism*,
ed. Richard H. Schwartz

He received the Sabbath with sweet song and chanted the hallowing tunefully over the wine . . . The table was well spread with all manner of fruit, beans, greenstuffs and good pies . . . but of flesh and fish there was never a sign . . . The old man and his wife had never tasted flesh since reaching maturity.
S. J. AGNON, *The Bridal Canopy*

Feed your animals before you sit down to eat.
TALMUD: BERAKOTH 40a

If the Torah had not been given at Sinai, we would have learned modesty from the cat, honesty from the ant, chastity from the dove, and good manners from the rooster who first coaxes, then mates.
BABYLONIAN TALMUD: ERUVIN 100b

Our rabbis said:
Even those things that you may regard
as completely superfluous to Creation—
such as fleas, gnats, and flies—
even they too were included in Creation;
and God's purpose is carried out through everything—
even through a snake, a scorpion, a gnat, or a frog.
GENESIS RABBAH 10:7

Lest I slight any creature, I must also mention the domestic animals, the beasts, and the birds from whom I have learned. Job said long ago (35:11): "Who teacheth us more than the beasts of the earth, and maketh us wiser than the fowls of heaven?" Some of what I have learned from them I have written in my books, but I fear that I have not learned as much as I should have done, for when I hear a dog bark, or a bird twitter, or a cock crow, I do not know whether they are thanking me for all I have told of them or calling me to account.

from S. J. Agnon's speech on receiving the Nobel Prize for Literature, in *Judaism and Vegetarianism*, ed. Richard H. Schwartz

God tested Moses through sheep.

When Moses tended the flock of his father-in-law, Jethro, one young kid ran away. Moses followed it until it reached a shaded area where it found a pool of water. There it stopped to drink.

Moses approached it and said, "I did not know you ran away because you were thirsty. Now you must be weary." So he placed the kid on his shoulders and carried it back.

Then God said, "Because you showed mercy in leading the flock of a mortal, you will surely show mercy in tending my flock, Israel."

EXODUS RABBAH 2:2

In Africa, two men stand at a river which they are about to cross, when they notice crocodiles looking at them. "Are you afraid?" says one to the other. "Don't you know that God is merciful and good?" "Yes, I do," says the frightened man. "But what if God suddenly chooses right now to be good to the crocodiles?"

ELIE WIESEL, *Sages and Dreamers*

For Lo! The winter is past, the rain is over and gone; the flowers appear on the earth, the time of singing has come, and the voice of the turtledove is heard in our land; the fig tree puts forth its figs and the vines are in blossom, they give forth fragrance.

SONG OF SONGS 2:11–13

The best remedy for those who are afraid, lonely, or unhappy is to go outside, somewhere where they can be quite alone with the heavens, nature, and God. Because only then does one feel that all is as it should be and that God wishes to see people happy, amidst the simple beauty of nature. As long as this exists, and it certainly always will, I know that there will always be comfort for every sorrow . . . And I firmly believe that nature brings solace in all troubles.

ANNE FRANK, *The Diary of a Young Girl*, 15 July 1944

THE HOLOCAUST

MY NIECE ELANA SHARED the following with her guests at her bat mitzvah celebration:

"The Holocaust is a big part of my family history. My name, Elana Sarah, is in memory of two relatives I never met who were killed by the Nazis during World War II. My grandpa Joe came from a family with five siblings. The oldest was Sarah. Sarah married before the war and had two children. One was a little girl named Helena, who was about four or five years old when the war broke out. Among the handful of black-and-white family pictures that survived the war is one of Sarah and her husband seated on the balcony of their apartment in the Warsaw suburb of Falenca, with the little blonde-haired Helena standing between them. The picture was taken in 1937. Who would have imagined that within a few short years, the three of them would be carted off and murdered in the Treblinka death camp. And not just them, my grandpa's parents too . . ."

Elana then focused on her grandfather's courage and dramatic survival during that period—he went on to save himself and four family members by jumping from a moving train that was routed for the death camp, Belzice. Later, imprisoned in Auschwitz, he again risked his life when he passed loaves of bread through barbed wire to women who were starving on the other side of the camp. And here he was, sitting in a shul in Shaker Heights, Cleveland, listening proudly to one of his six beautiful grandchildren recounting an incredibly heroic story that was his life.

Today, millions of children carry the names and thus the legacy of relatives lost during the greatest nightmare in Jewish history. They continue to tell the stories and in so doing, keep the memories alive. Literature and film have helped to imagine the unimaginable.

In some ways, I feel unqualified to address the Holocaust. I do not light a candle with my children at a Yom HaShoah service (the memorial services for loved ones who perished in the Holocaust). My husband and I both come from families that were spared the horrors. Our families emigrated from Russia many generations ago. Our connection is once removed, based either on the personal accounts of friends, teachers, and neighbors and their stories of grandparents, aunts, and uncles they never met. I vividly recall the fascination and sadness I felt as a teenager, each time I entered the kosher butcher or bakery on Broadway, waiting for a glimpse of numbers on the arms of familiar salespeople.

Whatever my qualifications, I realize that we are all connected, all accountable for one another, all responsible for repeating the stories and honoring the dead. Since this is a book of memories, the memory of those who perished must be preserved for eternity and the writings of those who lived through the horrors must be etched in the collective memory of all mankind.

For every anguished voice on these pages, there are thousands more just as powerful . . . and six million more we will never hear.

O THE CHIMNEYS

Nelly Sachs

O the chimneys
On the ingeniously devised habitations of death
When Israel's body drifted as smoke
Through the air—
Was welcomed by a star, a chimney sweep,
A star that turned black
Or was it a ray of sun?

O the chimneys!
Freedomway for Jeremiah and Job's dust—
Who devised you and laid stone upon stone
The road for refugees of smoke?

O the habitations of death,
Invitingly appointed
For the host who used to be a guest—
O you fingers
Laying the threshold
Like a knife between life and death—

O you chimneys,
O you fingers
And Israel's body as smoke through the air!

Liana Millu was an Italian Jewish journalist and novelist. She was arrested at twenty-four in Venice. She survived Birkenau and wrote Smoke over Birkenau *as an "outlet and liberation." Her book includes the powerful testimonies of six women who were there.*

Since our barrack was at the far end of the camp, right beside a crematorium, the auxiliary always got to us last. The guards took advantage of the extra time to give out the bread while we waited, which had its good and bad points: good because we were spared waiting in another line after roll-call, and bad because it was torture to get through the hour or hours of inspection with my bread under my arm. Each evening became an endurance test as I wrestled with the most ferocious temptation. I would start out full of resolve, hiding the bread inside my dress for a quarter of an hour or so, then take it out to gaze lovingly and sniff with passion, until the struggle between desire and the wisdom of deferred gratification culminated in my ripping into the bread like a starving beast, destroying in no time what was the object of endless inner conflict.
("Lili Marlene")

... I thought of what the crazy old woman had said. Maybe she was right after all, and Maria was actually pregnant. But what was the point of concealing it? Simply to have the baby at all costs? The more I pondered, the more her behavior seemed utterly selfish. Of course she wanted to give birth, it was an irresistible law of nature—but were the laws of nature still valid in a death camp? She refused to sacrifice her right to be a mother, refused the pain of having the child stripped from her, but why give birth to a creature who was doomed to feed the flames?
("Under Cover of Darkness")

It was the same old routine, putting one foot in front of the other. Everything is forever the same in the lager, pitilessly, hopelessly the same; each hour brings the same acts, the same commands, the same everything, until soon even your thoughts take the same predictable track, making the same fixed stops—

the war, home, getting back—a chronic sameness that becomes a torture worthy of Dante. At a certain bend in the road I would see a clump of grass sprouting between two rocks; it took fifty steps to get there. Each day, twice a day. I counted the steps and looked for the grass, and then I looked at the little poplars along the wide, well-trodden Lagerstrasse and thought invariably of how few of the people who had planted them two or three years ago were still around to watch their young leaves stirring.
("Scheiss Egal")

Along the way I kept glancing down at my pocket, where Gustine's treasure was hidden, and imagining what those cigarettes could mean to me in terms of food. One cigarette was worth six or seven potatoes, plus half a ration of bread. If I took just a handful, I'd have three or four bowlfuls of delicious hot yellow potatoes, maybe with a little onion. Anyone who has ever been in a lager, condemned to turnip soup, knows the kind of agonized yearning this image can call forth.
("Scheiss Egal")

... the great benefit of being prepared for the worst is that the merely bad always seems a blessing.
("Scheiss Egal")

Yaffa Eliach was my teacher in Camp Massad and remains to this day an outspoken poetic voice of the Holocaust. She is a petite, beautiful woman who lived through its horrors. Her baby brother was shot in their mother's arms just before their mother, who had begged to be killed first.

This story is based on a conversation of the Grand Rabbi of Bluzhov, Rabbi Israel Singer, with Aaron Frankel and Baruch Singer, June 22, 1975, which she heard at the rabbi's house.

The First Hanukkah Light in Bergen Belsen

In the Bergen Belsen, on the eve of Hanukkah, a selection took place. Early in the morning, three German commandants, meticulously dressed in their festive black uniforms and in visibly high spirits, entered the men's barracks. They ordered the men to stand at the foot of their three-tiered bunk beds.

The selection began. No passports were required, no papers were checked, there was no roll call and no head count. One of the three commandants just lifted the index finger in his snow-white glove and pointed in the direction of a pale face, while his mouth pronounced the death sentence with one single word: "Come!"

. . . The random selection went on inside the barracks and the brutal massacre continued outside of the barracks until sundown. When the Nazi black angels of death departed, they left behind heaps of hundreds of tortured and twisted bodies.

Then Hanukkah came to Bergen Belsen. It was time to kindle the Hanukkah lights. A jug of oil was not to be found, no candle was in sight. Instead, a wooden clog, the shoe of one of the inmates, became a hanukkiah; strings pulled from a concentration-camp uniform, a wick; and the black camp shoe polish, pure oil.

Not far from the heaps of the bodies, the living skeletons assembled to participate in the kindling of Hanukkah lights.

The Rabbi of Bluzhov lit the first light and chanted the first two blessings in his pleasant voice, and the festive melody was filled with sorrow and pain. When he was about to recite the third blessing, he stopped, turned his head, and looked around as if he were searching for something.

But immediately, he turned his face back to the quivering small lights and in a strong, reassuring, comforting voice, chanted the third blessing: "Blessed art Thou, O Lord our God, King of the Universe, who has kept us alive, and hast preserved us, and enabled us to reach this season."

Among the people present at the kindling of the lights was a Mr. Zamietchkowski, one of the leaders of the Warsaw Bund. He was a clever, sincere person with a passion for discussing matters of religion, faith, and truth. Even here in camp at Bergen Belsen, his passion for discussion did not abate . . .

As soon as the Rabbi of Bluzhov had finished the ceremony of kindling the lights, Zamietchkowski elbowed his way to the rabbi and said, "Spira, you are a clever and honest person. I can understand you need to light Hanukkah candles in these wretched times. I can even understand the historical note of the second blessing, 'Who wroughtest miracles for our fathers in days of old, at this season.' But the fact that you recited the third blessing is beyond me. How could you thank God and say 'Blessed are Thou, O Lord our God, King of the Universe, who has kept us alive, and hast preserved us, and enabled us to reach this season'? How could you say it when hundreds of dead Jewish bodies are literally lying within the shadows of the Hanukkah lights, when thousands of living Jewish skeletons are walking around in camp, and millions more are being massacred? For this you are thankful to God? For this you praise the Lord? This you call 'keeping us alive'?"

"Zamietchkowski, you are a hundred percent right," answered the rabbi. "When I reached the third blessing, I also hesitated and asked myself, what should I do with this blessing? I turned my head in order to ask the Rabbi of Zaner and other distinguished rabbis who were standing near me, if indeed I might recite the blessing. But just as I was turning my head, I noticed that behind me a throng was standing, a large crowd of living Jews, their faces expressing faith, devotion, and concentration as they were listening to the rite of the kindling of the Hanukkah lights. I said to myself, if God, blessed be He, has such a nation that at times like these, when during the lighting of the Hanukkah lights they see in front of them the heaps of bodies of their beloved fathers, brothers, and sons, and death is looking from every corner, if despite all that, they stand in throngs and with devotion listening to the Hanukkah blessing 'Who wroughtest miracles for our fathers in days of old, at this season'; if, indeed, I was blessed to see such a people with so much faith and fervor, then I am under a special obligation to recite the third blessing."

Some years after liberation, the Rabbi of Bluzhov, now residing in Brooklyn, New York, received regards from Mr. Zamietchkowski. Zamietchkowski asked the son of the Skabiner Rabbi to tell Israel Spira, the Rabbi of Bluzhov, that the answer he gave him that dark Hanukkah night in Bergen Belsen had stayed with him ever since, and was a constant source of inspiration during hard and troubled times.

YAFFA ELIACH, *Hasidic Tales of the Holocaust*

Primo Levi was arrested by Italian fascists in 1943 and deported from his native Turin to Auschwitz. He wrote many wonderful books and sadly, committed suicide in 1987. Survival in Auschwitz is his account of the "systematic cruelty and miraculous endurance" in the Nazi death camp.

We fought with all our strength to prevent the arrival of winter. We clung to all the warm hours, at every dusk we tried to keep the sun in the sky for a little longer, but it was all in vain . . .

We know what it means because we were here last winter; and the others will soon learn. It means that in the course of these months, from October till April, seven out of ten of us will die. Whoever does not die will suffer minute by minute, all day, every day: from the morning before dawn until the distribution of the evening soup we will have to keep our muscles continually tensed, dance from foot to foot, beat our arms under our shoulders against the cold. We will have to spend bread to acquire gloves, and lose hours of sleep to repair them, to eat in the open, we will have to eat our meals in the hut, on our feet, everyone will be assigned an area of floor as large as a hand, as it is forbidden to rest against the bunks. Wounds will open in every-one's hands, and to be given a bandage will mean waiting every evening for hours on one's feet in the snow and wind . . .

Just as our hunger is not that feeling of missing a meal, so our way of being cold has need of a new word. We say "hunger," we say "tiredness," "fear," "pain," we say "winter" and they are different things. They are free words, created and used by free men who lived in comfort and suffering in their homes. If the Lagers had lasted longer a new, harsh language would have been born; and only this language could express what it means to toil the whole day in the wind, with the temperature below freezing, wearing only a shirt, underpants, cloth jacket and trousers, and in one's body nothing but weakness, hunger and knowledge of the end drawing nearer . . .

Although we do not think for more than a few minutes a day, and then in a strangely detached and external manner, we well know that we will end in selections. I know that I am not made of the stuff of those who resist, I am too civilized, I still think too much, I use myself up at work. And now I also know that I can save myself if I become a Specialist, and that I will become a Specialist if I pass a chemistry examination . . .

To sink is the easiest of matters; it is enough to carry out all the orders one receives, to eat only the ration, to observe the discipline of the work and the camp. Experience showed that only exceptionally could one survive more than three months in this way. All the musselmans who finished in the gas chambers have the same story, or more exactly have no story; they followed the slope down to the bottom, like streams that run down to the sea. On their entry into the camp, through basic incapacity, or by misfortune, or through some banal incident, they are overcome before they can adapt themselves; they are beaten by time, they do not begin to learn German, to disentangle the infernal knot of laws and prohibitions until their body is already in decay, and nothing can save them from selections or from death by exhaustion. Their life is short, but their number is endless; they, the Muselmanner, the drowned, form the backbone of the camp, an anonymous mass, continually renewed and always identical, of non-men who march and labour in silence, the divine spark dead within them, already too empty to really suffer. One hesitates to call them living: one hesitates to call their death death, in the face of which they have no fear, as they are too tired to understand.

They crowd my memory with their faceless presences, and if I could enclose all the evil of our time in one image, I would choose this image which is familiar to me: an emaciated man, with head dropped and shoulders curved, on whose face and whose eyes not a trace of a thought is to be seen . . .
PRIMO LEVI, Survival in Auschwitz

Gisella Perl was a Hungarian Jew, an obstetrician and gynecologist who practiced medicine in her hometown of Sighet. In 1944, she was deported to Auschwitz-Birkenau where she was forced to work in the hospital with Dr. Mengele. Gisella Perl lost her whole family, but was liberated by the British in 1945. She worked in Sha'are Zedek Hospital in Israel and died in 1985.

The Value of a Piece of String

One day followed another in a horrible, nerve-racking monotony and the third month of my stay in Auschwitz arrived without my even being aware of it. We had long ago lost track of time, holding on in our minds to the past, the only escape from insanity. We sank deeper and deeper into the sub-human existence where filth, pain, and crime were natural, and a decent impulse, a human gesture, something to be sneered at and disbelieved. I knew that I had died on that March 19, when the Germans overran Hungary and compelled us to give up everything that meant anything to us, pushing us into a ghetto first, then robbing us of possessions, freedom and finally even of human dignity, in the seething, crawling, burning inferno. Here I was only a shadow without identity, alive only by the power of suffering.

It took a piece of string to shake me out of my apathy and remind me that while there was one single breath in me I could not permit myself to be engulfed in this swamp of human depravity.

For two months I had stood on my bare feet during the two daily roll calls. I had no shoes. My feet swelled up and were covered with sores—which was not only painful but also dangerous. Sore feet were reason enough for our Dr. Mengele to send us to the crematory. I had to have shoes . . . shoes at any price . . . Then one of the women working near the crematory stole a pair of shoes for me in exchange for two days' bread ration. Hunger was not new to me, in a way, I had become accustomed to it, and after only two months at Auschwitz my strength was still holding out—but shoes were a question of life and death.

I received a pair of men's shoes, about size ten, and I refused to listen when they tried to tell me the story of the man who had worn them, maybe not too long ago . . . I was happy. My aching feet were protected from the mud, the sharp gravel and the filth covering everything. They could rest in those shoes and heal in peace. But my happiness did not last long. The shoes were so big and I could not walk in them. I needed shoe strings. A piece of ordinary string. Anything to keep those shoes on my feet . . .

The thought of string filled my dreams and every minute of my waking hours. I wanted it so much, so desperately that nothing else seemed to matter anymore. A piece of string . . .

And then one of my acquaintances told me jubilantly that a few old prisoners, Polish men, were working around the latrines, and one of them had a piece of string . . . I snatched up my bread ration for the day and ran. The man with the string, my prospective savior, was a short, stocky, pockmarked man with wild eyes and a ferocious expression. The Inferno Auschwitz had succeeded in depriving him of his last vestige of human dignity.

I stopped beside him, held out my bread and asked him, begged him to give me a piece of string in exchange for it. He looked me over from head to foot, carefully, then grabbed me by the shoulder and hissed in my ear: "I don't want your bread . . . You can keep your bread . . . I will give you a piece of string but first I want you . . . you . . ."

For a second I didn't understand what he meant. I asked him again, smiling, gently, to give me a piece of string . . . My feet were killing me . . . The shoes were useless without string . . . It might save my life . . .

He wasn't listening to me. "Hurry up . . . hurry up . . ." he said hoarsely. His hand, filthy with the human excrement he was working in, reached out for my womanhood, rudely, insistently.

The next moment I was running, running away from that man, away from the indignity that had been inflicted on me, forgetting about the string, about the shoes, about everything but the sudden realization of how deeply I had sunk . . . How my values had changed . . . How high the price of a piece of string had soared . . .

I sank down on my bunk, dazed with suffering and fear . . . but a moment later I was on my feet again. No! I would not let this happen to me! I would come out of the apathy which had enveloped me for the last two months and show the Nazis, show my fellow prisoners that we would keep our human dignity in the face of every humiliation, every torture . . . Yes, I was going to remain a human being to the last minute of my life— whenever that would come.

The same evening, after retiring to our bunks, I began to put my plan into effect. Instead of going to sleep as usual, I began talking in a low voice to the women lying close to me. I told them about my old life in Maramaros Sziget, about my work, my husband, my son, the things we used to do, the books we used to read, the music we used to listen to . . . To my surprise they listened with rapt attention, which proved that their souls, their minds were just as hungry for conversation, for companionship, for self-expression as mine. One after the other, they opened up their hearts, and from then on half our nights were spent in conversation.

Later, as we came to know one another better, we invented games to keep our minds off the sordid present. We recited poetry, told stories of the books we had read and liked, and sang songs, in a low voice, with tears in our eyes, careful that the Blockova shouldn't hear us.

Other evenings we played another game, which spread from block to block until every woman in Auschwitz played it enthusiastically. We called the game "I am a lady . . ."

I am a lady—I said one night—a lady doctor in Hungary. It is morning, a beautiful, sunny morning and I feel too lazy to work. I ring for my assistant and tell her to send the patients away, for I am not going to my office today . . . What should I do with myself? Go shopping? Go to the hairdresser? Meet my friends at the café? Maybe I'll do some shopping. I haven't had a new dress, a new hat in weeks . . .

And I went shopping and lunching and walking, went to the theatre with my husband and son, had supper afterwards . . . And my fellow prisoners hung on my every word, following me around that little town they had never seen, and when my happy, lovely day was over, they fell asleep with a smile on their faces.

These evenings acted like a stimulant. They reminded us that although the odds were all against us, it was still our duty to fight. We had no longer homes to defend. All we had was our human dignity, which was our home, our pride, our only possession — and the moral strength to defend it with . . .

from "I Was a Doctor in Auschwitz" in *Different Voices*, ed. Card Ritter and John K. Roth

A DEAD CHILD SPEAKS
Nelly Sachs

My mother held me by my hand.
Then someone raised the knife of parting:
So that it should not strike me,
My mother loosed her hand from mine.
But she lightly touched my thighs once more
And her hand was bleeding —

After that the knife of parting
Cut in two each bite I swallowed —
It rose before me with the sun at dawn
And began to sharpen itself in my eyes —
Wind and water ground in my ear
And every voice of comfort pierced my heart —

And I was led to death
I still felt in the last moment
The unsheathing of the great knife of parting.

SHEMA

Primo Levi

You who live secure
In your warm houses,
Who return at evening to find
Hot food and friendly faces:

Consider whether this is a man,
Who labours in the mud
Who knows no peace
Who fights for a crust of bread
Who dies at a yes or a no.
Consider whether this is a woman,
Without hair or name
With no more strength to remember
Eyes empty and womb cold
As a frog in winter.

Consider that this has been:
I commend these words to you.
Engrave them on your hearts
When you are in your house, when you walk
    on your way,
When you go to bed, when you rise.
Repeat them to your children.
Or may your house crumble,
Disease render you powerless,
Your offspring avert their faces from you.

ISRAEL

I TRAVELED TO ISRAEL many times when I was a child without setting foot in the country. My earliest studies at a Jewish day school and later at Ramaz imbued me with its history, language, legends, and geography. I knew by heart the routes from Egypt to Canaan to the Red Sea and Jericho, the wars that were fought, the spies, the succession of kings, the family battles, the love affairs, and the miracles. At Camp Massad, nestled in the Pocono Mountains, my education continued and my imagination and spirit were further nourished. We spoke Hebrew among Israelis, performed plays in Hebrew, sang songs in praise of Israel's independence, and painted murals of kibbutzim and holy sites throughout the country. Israel's settlers, heroes, and poets were in our blood. In addition to the Beatles, our idols were Herzl, ben-Gurion, and Hannah Senesh.

Nothing, however, could prepare me for the first time I set foot on Israeli soil in the summer of 1968. The old city of Jerusalem with its beautiful light and unique stone, the Wailing Wall, the lush hills of the Galilee, the deserts, Masada, and the Dead Sea—I could finally see and smell and touch everything I had so long imagined.

Fueled by the freedom of being so far from home at age sixteen, I spent a month working on a kibbutz, the then traditional rite of passage for an American Jewish teenager. I would get up before dawn to feed the cows, clean the barn, or pick apples. I had a brief romance with a tall dark Sabra who drove a tractor. I witnessed the birth of a calf and ate the sweetest fruit in the world until I became ill. But more thrilling than any single event, I felt something happen inside of me: I was calm, comfortable, and excited all at once; I was home and proud of my Jewish roots.

I returned the following summer to explore the country further and work again on the kibbutz. I felt renewed joy, enthusiasm, and love for Israel (although the guy on the tractor was now in the army). One of the highlights of that summer was a concert in an ancient amphitheater among the ruins of Caesarea on the Mediterranean. I heard a young violinist named Itzhak Perlman play Bach's Second Brandenburg Concerto. When the concert concluded with the playing of "Hatikva" and the words "We have not lost our hope, a hope of two thousand years to be a free people in our land, in the land of Zion and Jerusalem," I was determined to spend the rest of my life in Israel. It was only a panicked and insistent phone call from my mother that forced me to return "temporarily" to New York.

The temporary return has now been extended twenty-eight years and counting. I have been back to Israel for brief visits many times since. At times I am upset that materialism has replaced the self-sacrifice of the pioneers. The conflict between Israel's right to exist in peace and security and the rights of the Palestinians takes an emotional toll on all supporters of Israel. Russian and Ethiopian immigrants have yet to be given the full measure of their citizenship and religious intolerance at both ends of the spectrum is staggering. But love for Israel is a little like a mother's love for her children. We hope and pray they will make good decisions and choose the right paths, but even when they seem to falter, we support them unconditionally.

Three years ago, my husband and I brought our children to Israel for their first visit. With the Bible as our guidebook, we toured and we watched as their history lessons fused with the antiquities and the countryside. Their enthusiasm and delight rekindled mine. But my children were not moved as I had been: The world is too changed. They will, I hope, discover its joys and riches privately. It is precisely their youth — their potential — that makes me optimistic that the very ideals that made Israel possible will flourish.

If you will it, it is not a dream.
THEODOR HERZL

If I forget you, O Jerusalem,
let my right hand wither
let my tongue stick to my palate
if I cease to think of you,
if I do not keep the destroyed city of Jerusalem in memory
even at my happiest hour.
PSALM 137:5–6

As long as the Jewish soul stirs within our heart,
And towards the East, to Zion, our eyes look with anticipation,
Then our hope is not yet lost — the hope of two thousand years —
To be a free people in our land, the land of Zion and Jerusalem.
N. H. IMBER, "Hatikva" (the Jewish National Anthem)

The people's heart is the foundation on which the land will be built.
ACHAD HA'AM

The State of Israel . . . will foster the development of the country for the benefit of all its inhabitants; it will be based on freedom, justice and peace as envisaged by the prophets of Israel; it will ensure complete equality of social and political rights to all of its inhabitants irrespective of religion, race or sex; it will guarantee freedom of religion, conscience, language, education and culture.

ISRAELI DECLARATION OF INDEPENDENCE

I don't know whether I've already mentioned that I've become a Zionist. This word stands for a tremendous number of things. To me it means, in short, that I now consciously and strongly feel I am a Jew, and am proud of it. My primary aim is to go to Palestine, to work for it. Of course this did not develop from one day to the next; it was a somewhat gradual development. There was first talk of it about three years ago, and at that time I vehemently attacked the Zionist movement. Since then people, events, times, have all brought me closer to the idea, and I am immeasurably happy that I've found this ideal, that I now feel firm ground under my feet, and can see a definite goal toward which it is really worth striving. I'm going to learn Hebrew, and I'll attend one of the youth groups. In short, I'm really going to knuckle down properly. I've become a different person, and it's a very good feeling.

One needs something to believe in, something for which one can have whole-hearted enthusiasm. One needs to feel that one's life has meaning, that one is needed in this world. Zionism fulfills all this for me. One hears a good many arguments against the Movement, but this doesn't matter. I believe in it, and that's the important thing.

I'm convinced Zionism is Jewry's solution to its problems, and that the outstanding work being done in Palestine is not in vain.

HANNAH SENESH'S DIARY, October 27, 1938, *Hannah Senesh: Her Life and Diary*

MY HEART IS IN THE EAST
Judah Halevi

My heart is in the East and I am at the
edge of the West. Then how can I taste
what I eat, how can I enjoy it? How
can I fulfill my vows and pledges
while Zion is in the domain of Edom,
and I am in the bonds of Arabia? It
would be easy for me to leave behind
all the good things of Spain; it would
be glorious to see the dust of the
ruined Shrine.

Within a single lifetime we have passed from a world in which
the existence of an independent Israel seemed inconceivable
into a world which seems inconceivable without its existence. I
know of few more tangible testimonies in history to the power
of the human will to assert itself against material odds. This is,
perhaps, the primary value of Israel's rebirth to all those who are
concerned with the vindication of faith against the fatalistic or
deterministic theories of history, which sees the human being
not as the primary agent of historic processes but merely as their
helpless subject matter . . . Now this belief in the human will is
a recurrent theme in Israel's history. The most distinctive attrib-
ute of Israel's character, the source of some weakness but of
greater strength, is this stubborn, tenacious refusal to recognize
the distinction between imagination and reality . . . This deliberate confusion between imagination and reality marks all our
religion and folklore.
ABBA EBAN, *A Modern Treasury of Jewish Thoughts*,
ed. Sidney Greenberg

Zionism was the Sabbath of my life. I believe that my influence as a leader is based on the fact that while as man and writer I had so many faults, and committed so many blunders and mistakes, as a leader in Zionism I have remained pure of heart and quite selfless.

It is marvelous how far my thoughts reach out when I awake too early in the morning. Then I solve many of the problems of the present, and glimpse some of the problems of eternity.

THEODOR HERZL, *Diaries*

We who belong to a people that has suffered more than any other, that has been uprooted from its soil, and alienated in unique fashion from nature, and that, on the other hand, still maintains the strength to survive despite two millennia of oppression—we understand, that in our striving for complete regeneration, we have no choice but to base the life we seek wholly upon its natural foundation. We must return fully to nature, to work, to creativity, and to a sense of order and spirituality characteristic of family-nationhood. More than others we must be concerned, indeed we are charged with the responsibility for the regeneration of our nation and for directing its attention to the development of the human spirit and the search for truth and righteousness in its relations with other peoples and with all mankind.

A. D. GORDON, "Fundamentals"

The spirit of the new life, of new creativeness, must penetrate labor and industry. The builder, the carpenter, the tailor, the factory worker, and so on, must first of all realize that he is a living being whose spiritual needs are as vital to him as his physical demands. He must feel that he and the others for whom he is working are bound not alone by economic ties, but by a spiritual, human bond. Like us, the farmers, he must strive toward the goal wherein the important thing for him must be not the

wage he receives for his work, but the work itself—the product of his labor. For this product is created to fill a vital need, physically, spiritually. Do we not see that while he is producing his wares for others that those others are laboring to fulfill his needs?
A. D. GORDON, "Fundamentals"

I believe that a wondrous generation of Jews will spring into existence. The Maccabees will rise again. Let me repeat once more my opening words: The Jews wish to have a state, and they shall have one. We shall live at last as free men on our own soil, and die peacefully in our own home. The world will be freed by our liberty, enriched by our wealth, magnified by our greatness. And whatever we attempt there to accomplish for our own welfare will react with beneficent force for the good of humanity.
THEODOR HERZL, *The Jewish State*

The Jews are a tiny people. Palestine is a tiny land. But when the tiny people will be reunited with the tiny land great things will come to pass.
MANAHEM USSISHKIN

The love of Eretz Yisroel was the torch that illuminated the thorny path of our people. It was the anchor that kept our ship from drifting out into the boundless ocean. And when the eternal wanderer seemed to sink under the burden of his suffering, he looked up into the sky and saw the light that shone from Zion, and with renewed courage he continued on his journey.
ISRAEL FRIEDLANDER, *Past and Present*

Jewish history in our lifetime will forever be dominated by this most fantastic transition from the depths of paralyzing despair to unexpected pinnacles of sovereignty, pride, and achievement.

Never was this people stronger than in its moment of weakness, never more hopeful than in its hour of despair.
ABBA EBAN, Address, 1952

I do not bring you a new idea but an immemorial one. Yes, it is a universal idea—and therein lies its strength—old as our people which never even in the days of its bitterest need ceased to nourish it. This idea is that of the foundation of the Jewish State. It is extraordinary that through the long night of our history we Jews continue to dream this regal dream . . . We plan for our posterity even as our fathers preserved the tradition for us.
THEODOR HERZL, *The Jewish State*

Faith in Israel means faith in the spiritual strength of the world.
NAHMAN SYRKIN

During two thousand years of our march through the wilderness the song of Israel has wallowed with us like the legendary well of Miriam—at times appearing, at times hiding; it has scarcely refreshed our soul, it has never satiated our thirst. And still, be that poetry blessed! It was the song of Israel which kept us in existence, which gave us vision and comfort.

Now a generation of youngsters jumps in with a new song in hand, and Israel, the gray old-aged, leans on his staff, bows his ear and listens with his heart palpitating to that far voice—the voice of the future. Their ideas and their way of speech do not always conform with his mind, but he is aware of their loyal allegiance, of their thorough Jewishness, and thinks:

"Heaven knows, maybe these youngsters carry in their hands the tonic, the juvenile vigor for their old aged people, maybe they will reerect its stature and adorn its gray head with a crown of honor and splendor."
CHAIM NACHMAN BIALIK, *Our Young Poetry*

PERHAPS
Rachel

Perhaps it was never so.
Perhaps
I never woke early and went to the fields
To labor in the sweat of my brow.

Nor in the long, blazing days
Of harvest
On top of the wagon, laden with sheaves,
Made my voice rise in song.

Nor bathed my self clean in the calm
Blue water
Of my Kineret, O, my Kineret,
Were you there or did I only dream?

MAN IS NOTHING BUT
Saul Tchernichovsky

Man is nothing but the soil of a small
    country,
nothing but the shape of his native
    landscape,
nothing but what his ears recorded
when they were new and really heard,
what his eyes saw, before they had their
    fill of seeing—
everything a wondering child comes
    across
on the dew-softened paths,

stumbling over every lump of earth,
    every old stone,
while in a hidden place in his soul,
    unknown to him,
there's an altar set up
from which the smoke of his sacrifice
    rises each day
to the kingdom of the sky, to the stars,
to the houses of the Zodiac.
But when the days become many, and in
    the war of being
the scroll of this Book of Life is being
    interpreted —
then comes, one by one, each letter with
    its interpretation
and each symbol revealing past and
    future
that was inscribed in it when it was first
    opened.
A man is nothing but the landscape of
    his homeland.

HEAVENLY JERUSALEM, JERUSALEM OF THE EARTH

Leah Goldberg

1

Divide your bread in two,
heavenly Jerusalem, Jerusalem of the Earth,
jewels of thorn on your slopes
and your sun among the thistles.
A hundred deaths rather than your mercy!

Divide your bread in two,
one half for the birds of the sky:
the other,
for heavy feet to trample
at the crossroads.

2

People are walking in the counterfeit city
whose heavens passed like shadows,
and no one trembles.
Sloping lanes conceal the greatness of her
    past.

The children of the poor
sing with indifferent voices:
"David, King of Israel, lives and is."

3
Over my house
one late swallow.
All the other swallows
have already returned to the north.
Over my head
towards evening,
in a city
weary of wanderings
in a city of wanderers,
small trembling wings
trace circles of despair.

A sky of Hebron glass.
The first lamp of night.
Swallow with no nest.
Arrested flight.

What now?

My parents who came from another country sought to make the Israel of their imagination, drawn from descriptions in the Bible, their physical homeland. In somewhat the reverse way, I sought to give my real and tangible homeland the added dimension of historical depth, to bring to life the strata of the past which now lay beneath the desolate ruins and archeological mounds—the Israel of our patriarchs, our judges, our kings, our prophets.

MOSHE DAYAN, *Living with the Bible*

I believe there is a solution to the Arab-Israeli conflict, and if we cannot find it, then I consider Zionism has failed utterly.

HENRIETTA SZOLD commenting on the political situation in Palestine during the 1930s in *Great Jewish Quotations*, ed. Alfred J. Kolatch

I'm an old guy. I served twenty-seven years in the military. My son served. Now my grandson serves. Let's give a hope that at least my grandson will not need to fight. If there will be a need, I'm sure that a fourth generation also will do it. But I feel a responsibility to give a chance that it will not happen.

YITZHAK RABIN in a statement made in Jerusalem on September 11, 1993, before leaving for the United States to sign a peace treaty with the PLO in *Great Jewish Quotations*, ed. Alfred J. Kolatch

We should not let the land flowing with milk and honey become the land flowing with blood and tears.

YITZHAK RABIN in a speech at the White House, September 28, 1995

The difficult we do immediately. The impossible takes a little longer.

DAVID BEN-GURION

Let me tell you something we have against Moses. He took us forty years through the desert in order to bring us to the one spot in the Middle East that has no oil.
GOLDA MEIR in 1973

I said to my colleagues, "*Surrender?* What is this word surrender? It has no meaning in Hebrew!" Then I went to the lavatory to vomit.
GOLDA MEIR in an interview toward the end of her life

When peace comes, we will perhaps in time be able to forgive the Arabs for killing our sons, but it will be harder for us to forgive them for having forced us to kill their sons.
GOLDA MEIR in an interview after the Six-Day War, 1967

THE NEW EZEKIEL

Emma Lazarus

What, can these dead bones live, whose sap is dried
    By twenty scorching centuries of wrong?
Is this the House of Israel whose pride
    Is a tale that's told, an ancient song?
Are these ignoble relics all that live
    Of psalmist, priest and prophet? Can the
        breath
Of very heaven bid these bones revive,
    Open the graves and clothe the ribs of death?

Yea, Prophesy, the Lord hath said. Again
    Say to the wind, Come forth and breathe
        afresh,
Even that they may live upon these slain,
    And bone to bone shall leap, and flesh to
        flesh.

The Spirit is not dead, proclaim the word,
    Where lay dead bones, a host of armed men
        stand!
I ope your graves, my people, saith the Lord,
    And I shall place you living in your land.

Israel is to be compared to a sleeping giant, arising from the slough of despair and darkness and straightening up to his infinite height. His face is rimmed by rays of glory of the pain of the world which he has suffered . . . He knows his task, to do justice and proclaim truth. His tragic history has resulted in a high mission. He will redeem the world which crucified him.

NAHMAN SYRKIN, "The Jewish Problem and the Socialist Jewish State"

BLESSED IS THE MATCH

Hannah Senesh

Blessed is the match that is consumed in
    kindling the flame.
Blessed is the flame that burns in the secret
    fastness of the heart.
Blessed is the heart with strength to stop its
    beating for honor's sake.
Blessed is the match that is consumed in
    kindling the flame.

He who does not know exile will not understand how luridly it colors our sorrows, how it pours the darkness of night and poison into all our thoughts . . . Only he who has lived in exile knows what love of fatherland is—patriotism with all its sweet terrors and its nostalgic trials.

HEINRICH HEINE, *Ludwig Borne*

A State is not handed to a nation on a silver platter.
CHAIM WEIZMANN

THE SILVER PLATTER
Natan Alterman

. . . The earth grows still. The reddened eye of the
   heavens
Dims slowly out
Over smoke-shrouded borders.
And a nation stands — torn-hearted but breathing —
To receive the one miracle
Unlike any other.

Awaiting the ceremony: they arose to a crescent
And stand, before dawn, draped in celebration and dread.
— Then from afar there come forth
A youth and a maiden
And slowly towards the nation before them they tread.

Wearing drab and equipment, and heavily shod,
They walk up the path
Without even a whisper.
They haven't changed clothes, or used water and washed
The signs off of the harsh day and of the night under fire.

Weary past ending, hermits from repose,
And gleaming with the dew of Hebrew youth
They in silence approach
And motionless, pause.
And there's no way of knowing if they're alive or've been
   shot.

And the nation inquires, in tears and in wonder,
And says: Who are you? And soft speak the two,
And reply: We are the silver platter
Upon which the Jewish State is handed to you.

So speaking, they fall at the nation's feet, now their veil.
And the rest will be recounted in the annals of Israel.

DEATH AND MOURNING

THERE ARE VERY CLEAR guidelines in Jewish law about how to deal with death and mourning. The burial rites are very simple, enforcing the idea of "democracy in death" so that no family, however poor, shall be ashamed by the simplicity of coffin or shroud. Following the funeral, the family spends a week of shiva—seven days at home during which they can mourn and express their grief among family and friends, rather than repress it. During that week, the bereaved abstain from normal activities. Their needs are provided by friends and community. The Kaddish is recited for a year following the death of a parent and a Yahrzeit candle is lit every year on the anniversary of that person's death, as it is written in Proverbs, "The spirit of man is the candle of the Lord."

The Bible records many instances of tearing one's clothes upon hearing the news of a death. When Jacob saw his son Joseph's multicolored coat drenched in blood, he "rent his garments and placed sackcloth on his loins; he mourned for his son many days." (Genesis 37:34)

The mourner's garment is torn over the heart to represent a broken heart. In pagan religions, the flesh was torn or the hair pulled out, but Judaism forbids this. There is something very powerful about the image and the sound of a garment being torn. When I was twelve, my father died. I vividly recall my shirt being torn and those of my brother and sisters in turn, and a pain shot through my body with each tear. The memory of this ritual continues to move me whenever I witness it at a graveside — that and the first recital of the mourner's Kaddish. In some ways, the hollow left in our hearts can be filled with warm memories and the love we have for the person we have lost, but the broken heart is never fully restored. Judaism, however, teaches us that after a week of shiva and thirty days of less restricted behavior, we must return to our normal lives with the hope of understanding and accepting that death is a part of life. We move once again toward life, affirming our participation in it.

Have courage, no one is immortal.
JEWISH EPITAPH (ROME, C. 200 C.E.)

Man is like a breath, his days are like a passing shadow . . . So teach us to treasure our days that we may get a wise heart.
PSALMS 144:4, 90:12

God kissed Moses and took away his soul with a kiss of the mouth. And God wept.
LEGEND

And he made a mourning for his father seven days.
GENESIS 5:10

For dying, you always have plenty of time.
YIDDISH FOLK SAYING

In death, two worlds meet with a kiss: the world going out and the future coming in.

TALMUD: YEBAMOTH 57a

It is better to visit a house of mourning than a house of feasting.

ECCLESIASTES 7:2

All who pass by when one is buried must accompany the funeral procession and join in the lamentation.

JOSEPHUS, *Against Apion* II

alav ha-shalom (masculine)
aleha ha-shalom (feminine)

Pronounced aw-luv ha sha-LOAM or HA-luv ha SHO-lem (the first pronunciation is Hebrew, and elegant; the second is Yiddish, and brisk). The two Hebrew words are often pronounced as if one: alevasholem. The feminine form is aleha ha-shalom, pronounced ah-leh-ha ha-SHO-lem or SHA-loam.

Literally: "On him (or her) peace."

• • •

The phrase is used, automatically, when referring to someone who is dead—as, in English, one says "Of blessed memory," or "May he rest in peace."

When a man says, "My uncle Harry, alevasholem, once said . . ." you can be sure that Uncle Harry is dead.

As a boy, I was fascinated by the obligatory "alevasholem," but puzzled to hear: "That man? A liar, no-good, alevasholem." Thus realism, wrestling with ritual, resolves ambivalence. In fact, the primary purpose of ritual is to provide a routine for the management of emotion. Routine reduces anxiety by removing choices.

It also used to please me, as a boy, to hear a patriarch utter a fearsome oath thusly: "May beets grow in his belly! God forbid." It pleased me, I say, because "God forbid" took the edge off a malediction uttered in anger — *after* the anger had been healthily expressed.

Jews are at home with strong emotions. They express feelings with ease, to say nothing of eloquence, then politely dilute them — to be on the safe side of things.

• • •

It was at the great Café Royale, on Second Avenue in New York City, *alevasholem*, that I first heard this classic joke:

SCENE: *Restaurant.*

WAITER: "Tea or coffee, gentlemen?"

1ˢᵗ CUSTOMER: "I'll have tea."

2ⁿᵈ CUSTOMER: "Me, too — and be sure the glass is clean!"

(Waiter exits, returns)

WAITER: "Two teas. Which one asked for the clean glass?"

LEO ROSTEN, *The Joys of Yiddish*

New York, 16 September 1916

It is impossible for me to find words in which to tell you how deeply I was touched by your offer to act as *"kaddish"* for my dear mother. I cannot even thank you — it is something that goes beyond thanks. It is beautiful, what you have offered to do — I shall never forget it.

You will wonder, then, that I cannot accept your offer. Perhaps it would be best for me not to try to explain to you in writing, but to wait until I see you to tell you why it is so. I know well, and appreciate what you say about the Jewish custom; and Jewish custom is very dear and sacred to me. And yet I cannot ask you to say *Kaddish* after my mother. The *Kaddish* means to me that the survivor publicly and markedly manifests his wish and intention to assume the relation to the Jewish community which his parent had, and that so the chain of tradition remains unbroken from generation to generation, each adding its own link. You can do that for the generation of your family, I must do that for the generations of my family.

I believe that the elimination of women from such duties was never intended by our law and custom — women were freed from positive duties when they could not perform them, but not when they could. It was never intended that, if they could perform them, their performance of them should not be considered as valuable and valid as when one of the male sex performed them. And of the *Kaddish* I feel sure this is particularly true.

My mother had eight daughters and no son; and yet never did I hear a word of regret pass the lips of either my mother or father that one of us was not a son. When my father died, my mother would not permit others to take her daughters' place in saying the *Kaddish*, and so I am sure I am acting in her spirit when I am moved to decline your offer. But beautiful your offer remains nevertheless, and, I repeat, I know full well that it is much more in consonance with the generally accepted Jewish tradition than is my or my family's conception. You understand me, don't you?

HENRIETTA SZOLD from a letter to Haym Peretz in *Four Centuries of Jewish Women's Spirituality*, ed. Ellen M. Umansky and Dianne Ashton

She's dying. Mother is dying! I tried to think, to make myself realize that Mother, with all this dumb sorrow gazing at me, was passing, passing away, for ever. But above the dull pain that pressed on my heart, thinking was impossible. I felt I was in the clutch of some unreal dream from which I was trying to waken. Tiny fragments of memory rushed through my mind. I remembered with what wild abandon Mother had danced the *kozatzkeh* at a neighbor's wedding. With what passion she had bargained at the pushcart over a penny . . . How her face lit up whenever company came! How her eyes sparkled with friendliness as she served the glasses of tea, spread everything we had on the table, to show her hospitality. A new pair of stockings, a clean apron,

a mere car ride, was an event in her life that filled her with
sunshine for the whole day . . . Is there a God over us and sees
her suffer so? . . . She had seized me by the hand. She had
begged me to come and see her. And I had answered her, "I
can come to see you later, but I can't go to college later. . . ."
"Mamma — mamma!"
Suddenly the sorrowful eyes became transfigured with light.
Her lips moved. I could not get the words, but the love-light of
Mother's eyes flowed into mine. I felt literally Mother's soul
enter my soul like a miracle. Then all became dark.
ANZIA YEZIERSKA, *The Bread Givers*

But who is now my comforter? To whom shall I pour out my
soul? Whither shall I turn? All his life my beloved companion
hearkened to my troubles, and they were many, and comforted
me so that somehow they would quickly vanish. But now, alas,
I am left to flounder in my woe.
GLUCKEL OF HAMELN lamenting the death of her husband in
Gluckel of Hameln, *The Memoirs of Gluckel of Hameln*

AFTER MY DEATH
(excerpt)
Chaim Nahman Bialik

After I am dead
Say this at my funeral:
There was a man who exists no more.
That man died before his time
And his life's song was broken off halfway.
O, he had one more poem
And that poem has been lost
For ever.

It's not that I'm afraid to die. I just don't want to be there when it happens.
WOODY ALLEN, *Love and Death*

How Large Should a Cemetery Be?

After the Chelmites had completed their houses, they began to consider the problem of a cemetery. There was some suitable land available on the outskirts of the city, but they did not know precisely how large the cemetery should be. They didn't want it to be too large or too small. No, it must be exactly right.

The Chelmites were in session for several days and nights. They discussed and argued and weighed every proposal. Finally they reached this decision: let the whole community—men, women and children—leave the city and gather on the chosen site. Let every person lie down next to his neighbor, row by row, according to one's station and lineage: the most honored in the best parts of the site, the common people in the less desirable parts, the women in separate rows, and the children in the corner. Then a fence should be built around.

This they did. So the cemetery of Chelm was neither too large nor too small but exactly the right size.
The Jewish Caravan, ed. Leo Schwartz

We rejoice over a birth and mourn over a death. But we should not. For when a man is born, who knows what he will do or how he will end? But when a man dies, we may rejoice—if he left a good name and this world is in peace.
adapted from MIDRASH: TANHUMA ON EXODUS

Our sorrow can bring understanding as well as pain, breadth as well as the contraction that comes with pain. Out of love and sorrow can come a compassion that endures. The needs of other hitherto unnoticed, the anxieties of neighbors never before realized, now come into the ken of our experience, for our sorrow has opened our life to the needs of others. A bereavement that brings us into the lives of our fellowmen writes a fitting epilogue to a love that had taught us kindliness, and forbearance and had given us so much joy.

Sorrow can enlarge the domain of our life, so that we may now understand the triviality of the things many pursue. We have in our hands a noble and refined measure for judging the events and objects we daily see. What is important is not luxury but love; not wealth but wisdom; not gold but goodness . . .

Our sorrow may so clear our vision . . . [and] out of that vision will come a sense of obligation. A duty, solemn, sacred and significant, rests upon us. To spread the love we have known to others. To share the joy which has been ours. To ease the pains which man's thoughtlessness or malice inflicts. We have a task to perform. There is work to be done and in work there is consolation.

Out of love may come sorrow. But out of sorrow can come light for others who dwell in darkness. And out of the light we bring to others will come light for ourselves—the light of solace, of strength, of transfiguring and consecrating purpose.

MORRIS ADLER in *A Modern Treasury of Jewish Thoughts*, ed. Sidney Greenberg

No one gets accustomed to death. For instance, the owner of a funeral parlor—you might think that such a man is hardened enough to get accustomed to death. No. They get accustomed to other people's deaths, but they certainly don't get accustomed to the idea that they will die. This is true about every human being. The fear of death exists in every human being from childhood to the grave. The only time when people stop being afraid of death is when they die.

ISAAC BASHEVIS SINGER, *Conversations*

Undo it, take it back, make every day the previous one until I am returned to the day before the one that made you gone. Or set me on an airplane traveling west, crossing the date line again and again, losing this day, then that, until the day of loss still lies ahead, and you are here instead of sorrow.

NESSA RAPOPORT, *A Woman's Book of Grieving*

No answers at all. We find parts of answers, answers in certain circumstances, some personal answers. But the great answer to why we were born, why we are here, why we have to die, why we have to witness, and why we suffer, can never be answered in a really satisfying way. I would say that man is going to ask these questions to the very end of his existence.

ISAAC BASHEVIS SINGER, *Conversations*

Dear American friend, that miserable patch of event, that melange of nothing, while you were looking ahead for something to happen, that was it! That was life! You lived it!

CLIFFORD ODETS, *Clifford Odets, American Playwright, The Years from 1906–1940*

In Jewish tradition, it is customary to light a yahrzeit, *or memory candle, on the anniversary of a family member's death.*

> The *yahrzeit* flame
> is beating its wings in a cup
> on the edge of my kitchen sink.
> Its stealthy gold shadow
> breathing along the wall
> suddenly terrifies me:
> like finding a bird in my bedroom

still alive pulsating nervous,
changing the shape of the day.

No intruder is ever harmless.
And, Mother, I've got you cornered,
fierce memory pacing your glass cage,
houseguest with nowhere to go.
I'll lock myself in alongside you.
Today, we'll remind each other
of old connections, old journeys,
from muddy, sincere Indiana
to ragged-edged Brooklyn
with all its stray cats, its ecstatic
vegetable stands.
ENID DAME in *The Tribe of Deena*

Some who live are dead and there are those dead who still live.
PHILO

There are no bad mothers and no good death.
YIDDISH FOLK SAYING

The basis of wisdom is not in the reflection on death but in the
reflection on life.
BARUCH SPINOZA

On the day he dies every man feels he has lived only a single
day.
FOLK SAYING

If God didn't hide from all people the date of their death, nobody would build a home, nobody would plant a vineyard, because everyone would say, "I'm going to die tomorrow, so of
what purpose is it for me to work today?"

For this reason, God denies us knowing the day of our death, in the hope we will build and plant.

[If not us] others will benefit from our labor.

YALKUT SHIMONI on Ecclesiastes 968

Naked I came from my mother's womb and naked shall I return there.

JOB 1:21

Movie mogul Samuel Goldwyn once criticized Dorothy Parker: "Your stories are too sad, Dorothy. What the public wants are happy endings."

"Mr. Goldwyn," she responded. "Since the world was created, billions and billions of people have lived, and not a single one has had a happy ending."

from JOSEPH TELUSHKIN, *Jewish Wisdom*

It seems to me that the duty of comforting mourners takes precedence over the duty of visiting the sick, because comforting mourners is an act of benevolence toward the living and the dead.

MAIMONIDES, MISHNEH TORAH 14:7

It is indeed impossible to imagine our own death, and whenever we attempt to do so we can perceive that we are in fact still present as spectators . . . At bottom no one believes in his own death.

SIGMUND FREUD, "Thoughts for the Times on War and Death"

The Cemetery at Kozin

The cemetery of a little Jewish town. Assyria and all the mysterious stagnation of the East, over those weed-grown plains of Volhnyia.

Carved gray stones with inscriptions three centuries old. Crude high reliefs hewn out in the granite. Lambs and fishes depicted above a skull, and Rabbis in fur caps—Rabbis girt round their narrow loins with leather belts. Below their eyeless faces the rippling stone line of their curly beards. To one side, beneath a lightning-shattered oak, stands the burial vault of the Rabbi Azrael, slain by the Cossacks of Bogdan Khmelnitsky. Four generations lie buried in that vault that is as lowly as a water-carrier's dwelling; and the memorial stone, all overgrown with green, sings of them with the eloquence of a Bedouin's prayer.

"Azrael son of Ananias, Jehova's mouthpiece.

"Elijah son of Azrael, brain that struggled single-handed with oblivion.

"Wolff son of Elijah, prince robbed from the Torah in his nineteenth spring.

"Judah son of Wolff, Rabbi of Cracow and Prague.

"O death, O covetous one, O greedy thief, why couldst thou not have spared us, just for once?"

ISAAC BABEL, *The Collected Stories of Isaac Babel*

Beruriah lived in the second century and her wisdom and right-eousness were legendary even in her own time. She is the only woman whose views were considered seriously by Talmudic scholars. The following is the most famous story associated with her and it concerns the death of her two sons on the Sabbath, news she withheld from her husband until the end of the Sabbath.

Some time ago I was entrusted by a friend with some jewels for safekeeping and now he wants them back.

Shall I return them?

Of course, answered Rabbi Meir, the jewels must be returned.

Beruriah then took him to where their dead sons were lying.

When he collapsed and cried she gently reminded him: "Did you not say we must return to the owner the precious jewels he entrusted to us? The Lord has given, the Lord has taken away. Blessed be the name of the Lord."

BERURIAH, MIDRASH: PROVERBS 31:10, in *Written Out of History*, ed. Sondra Henry and Emily Taitz

In silence he was born, in silence he lived, in silence he died — and in an even vaster silence he was put into the ground.

Ah, but in the other world it was not so! No! In Paradise the death of Bontsha was an overwhelming event. The great trumpet of the Messiah announced through the seven heavens: Bontsha the Silent is dead! The most exalted angels, with the most imposing wings, hurried, flew, to tell one another, "Do you know who has died? Bontsha! Bontsha the Silent!"

And the new, the young little angels with brilliant eyes, with golden wings and silver shoes, ran to greet Bontsha, laughing in their joy. The sound of their wings, the sound of their silver shoes, as they ran to meet him, and the bubbling of their laughter, filled all Paradise with jubilation, and God Himself knew that Bontsha the Silent was at last here . . .

". . . No, for you there is everything! Whatever you want! Everything is yours!"

"Well then" — and Bontsha smiles for the first time — "well then, what I would like, Your Excellency, is to have every morning for breakfast, a hot roll with fresh butter."

A silence falls upon the great hall, and it is more terrible than Bontsha's has ever been, and slowly the judge and the angels bend their heads in shame at this unending meekness they have created on earth.

Then the silence is shattered. The prosecutor laughs aloud, a bitter laugh.

ISAAC L. PERETZ, "Bontsha the Silent," *Great Yiddish Stories*

Friends and relatives filed past the open coffin, sniffling and sighing. Mrs. Tannenbaum said to a friend, "You'd think he was just sleeping. Look at him — tan, relaxed . . . so healthy."
"Why shouldn't he be?" replied her friend.
"He just came back from two weeks in Miami."

There should be nothing astonishing in our facing death on behalf of our laws with a courage which no other nation can equal. For even those practices of ours which seem the easiest others find difficult to tolerate: I mean personal service, simple diet, discipline which leaves no room for freak or individual caprice in matters of meat and drink or in the sexual relations, or in extravagance or again the abstention from work at rigidly fixed periods . . . Our willing obedience to the law in these matters results in the heroism which we display in the face of death.

JOSEPHUS, *Against Apion* II: 231–236

I am formed of soul and body, I seem to have mind, reason, sense, yet I find that none of them is really mine. Where was my body before birth, and whither will it go when I have departed? What has become of the changes produced by life's various stages in the seemingly permanent self?

PHILO, *On the Cherubim* 110–114

What shall I do? Everyone wants to go to heaven, but nobody wants to die.

SAM LEVENSON

KADDISH
(excerpt)
Allen Ginsberg

Strange now to think of you, gone without corsets & eyes,
   while I
      walk on the sunny pavement of Greenwich Village,
downtown Manhattan, clear winter noon, and I've been up all
   night,
      talking, talking, reading the Kaddish aloud, listening to Ray
      Charles blues shout blind on the phonograph
the rhythm—and your memory in my head three years
      after—And read Adonais' last triumphant stanzas aloud—
      wept, realizing how we suffer—
And how Death is that remedy all singers dream of, sing,
   remember,
      prophesy as in the Hebrew Anthem, or the Buddhist Book of
      Answers—and my own imagination of a withered leaf—at
      dawn . . .
This is the end, the redemption from Wilderness, way for the
Wonderer, House sought for All, black handkerchief washed clean
by weeping—page beyond Psalm—Last change of mine and Naomi—to God's perfect Darkness—Death, stay thy phantoms!

You know what would be a nice way to kill a day? I think it would
be nice to take a trip up to Mount Hope Cemetery and have a look
at my burial plot. A lovely cemetery. Like a golf course, actually.
By the time one gets there and comes back, the whole day has
been used up. Would you like to come? I'll pay both your fares.
PADDY CHAYEFSKY, *The Tenth Man*

Death cannot be and is not the end of life. Man transcends death
in many altogether naturalistic fashions. He may be immortal
biologically, through his children, in thought through the sur-

vival of his memory; in influence, by virtue of the continuance of his personality as a force among those who came after him, and, ideally, through his identification with the timeless things of the spirit. When Judaism speaks of immortality, it has in mind all these. But its primary meaning is that man contains something independent of the flesh and surviving it; his consciousness and moral capacity; his essential personality; a soul.

MILTON STEINBERG, *Basic Judaism*

There are stars whose radiance is visible on earth though they have long been extinct. There are people whose brilliance continues to light the world though they are no longer among the living. These lights are particularly bright when the night is dark.

HANNAH SENESH's final words to her comrades before she was executed by firing squad, November 1944

The meaning of life is that it stops.

FRANZ KAFKA

WISDOM AND LEARNING

The important thing is not to stop questioning.
ALBERT EINSTEIN

THE REVERENCE FOR KNOWLEDGE, education, and wisdom among Jews is legendary. From biblical times on, it was the obligation of *all* Jews to study and question. Moses ordered the elders of Israel to "gather the people — men, women, and children, and the strangers in your communities — that they may hear and so learn." It is noteworthy that the epithet we attach to Moses, our most important historical figure, is not redeemer or leader but "Rabbenu," our teacher. For Jews that has been the highest commendation.

The Talmud, a compilation of a thousand years of Jewish oral traditions, ethical teachings, and analyses of every detail of biblical law, teaches us as much about how to learn as what to learn. We are encouraged to probe, argue, consider every thought from every perspective. Like any book that we read and reread, we always find something new, something fresh. We develop our minds, hone our skills by learning how to question. The Talmud challenges every Jew to explore, define, and redefine what makes us Jews.

Both my husband and I were raised in homes devoted to education. The lessons, the inquiries, and the call for excellence began early and in earnest. Our parents knew, as theirs did, that knowledge would bring us into the world as better people, better Jews, and better able to do good. Along with our work, that process has continued with extracurricular studies as diverse as nature courses (albeit in Central Park), Italian conversation, Talmud, speed swimming, and our mutual addiction to the pleasures of reading. The resources are endless—music, films, conversations with close friends, and the learning experience in raising four children. If we can pass on to them not only our love but our love for learning, then we will consider ourselves successful. What they do with it will be up to them.

Wisdom is more than the sum total of our accumulated knowledge. It is that mystical union of experience, understanding, insight, and humanity. We seek the counsel of the wise for clarity, guidance, encouragement, and solace. Wisdom's exemplar, King Solomon, asked for God's help to lead his people.

God appeared to Solomon and said to him, "Ask what I shall give you." And Solomon said to God, "You have shown great kindness to David, my father, and have made me king in his stead . . . Give me now wisdom and knowledge that I may go out and come in before this people; for who can judge these your people, that are so great?"
2 CHRONICLES 1:7–8

Because he did not seek riches or honor, the deaths of his enemies or long life for himself, God granted him everything. We are urged to pursue wisdom for ourselves and encourage its lessons in our children. But it is not the automatic legacy of study or even of old age, though we may secretly long for it as recompense for wrinkles. It is the sum of our deliberate choices and inevitable experiences. It is as unique as our personalities.

We do not receive wisdom, we must discover it for ourselves, after a journey through the wilderness which no one else can make for us, which no one can spare us, for our wisdom is the point of view from which we came last to regard the world.
MARCEL PROUST, *Within a Budding Grove*

Who is wise? He who learns from all men.
Ethics of the Fathers 4:1

My son eat thou honey, for it is good, And the honeycomb is sweet to thy taste; So know thou wisdom to be unto thy soul; If thou hast found it, then shall there be a future, And thy hope shall not be cut off.
PROVERBS 24:13–14

Only learning that is enjoyed will be learned well.
JUDAH HA-NASI

Through wisdom is a house built, And by understanding it is established; And by knowledge are the chambers filled with all precious and pleasant riches.
PROVERBS 24:3–4

Many wise words are spoken in jest, but they don't compare with the number of stupid words spoken in earnest.
SAM LEVENSON, *You Don't Have to Be in Who's Who to Know What's What*

At one time in Lithuania—perhaps not so much today—Torah was held in higher esteem than money. A boor, no matter how rich, was nothing more than a boor. Never would he be voluntarily accorded a place of honor or listened to open-mouthed. Oh, no! To be worthy of that, one had to be learned, good, pious, and come of a good family. Prestige depended not on the moneybags but upon the mind and the heart.

MENDELE MOKHER SFORIM, *How We Lived*, ed. Irving Howe and Kenneth Libo

A student should not be embarrassed if a fellow student has understood something after the first or second time and he has not grasped it even after several attempts. If he is embarrassed because of this, it will turn out that he will come and go from the house of study without learning anything at all.

Shulkhan Arukh, Yoreh De'ah 246:11

For wisdom is better than rubies; and all the things that may be desired are not to be compared to it.

PROVERBS 8:11

We must not indeed reject any learning that has grown grey through time, nay, we should make it our aim to read the writings of the sages and listen to proverbs and old-world stories from the lips of those who know antiquity, and ever seek for knowledge about the men and deeds of old. For truly it is sweet to leave nothing unknown.

PHILO, *The Sacrifices of Abel and Cain*

Acquire wisdom, acquire understanding; never forget nor depart from the words of my mouth.

PROVERBS 4:5

For God shall give wisdom,
out of His mouth comes knowledge and understanding;
and He has energy in store for the upright,
is a shield to them who walk in integrity,

to guard the paths of justice
and protect the ways of those lovingly dedicated to Him.
Then you will gain understanding of justice and order,
how straight is every good way.
Once wisdom has entered your heart
and knowledge is sweet to your soul,
reflection shall watch over you,
understanding shall guard you,
to deliver you from the way of evil,
from any man who speaks perversely.
PROVERBS 2:6–12

It's so simple to be wise. Just think of something stupid to say
and say the opposite.
SAM LEVENSON, *You Don't Have to Be in Who's Who to Know
What's What*

An understanding heart acquires knowledge, and the ear of the
wise seeks knowledge.
PROVERBS 18:15

Disciples increase the teacher's wisdom and broaden his mind.
The sages said, "Much wisdom I learned from my teachers, more
from my colleagues, from my pupils most of all." Even as a small
piece of wood kindles a large log, so a pupil of small attainment
sharpens the mind of his teacher, so that by his questions, he
elicits glorious wisdom.
MAIMONIDES, MISHNEH TORAH

There are four types among those who sit in the presence of
sages: the sponge, the funnel, the strainer and the sifter.
    The sponge soaks up everything.
    The funnel takes in at one ear and lets out at the other.

The strainer lets the wine pass and retains the dregs.
The sifter holds back the coarse and collects the fine flour.
Ethics of the Fathers 5:18

The two most precious gifts we can give our children are Roots
and Wings—to be firmly rooted in our rich Judaic Heritage, and
to be inspired to reach one's fullest potential.
RABBI JOSEPH H. LOOKSTEIN

Learning begins with listening.
NOAH BEN SHEA, *The Word*

To remember much is not necessarily to be wise.
SAMUEL DAVID LUZZATTO

One of the "wise men" of Chelm said to his wife, "If I were the
czar, I would be even richer than the czar."
  "How is that possible?" asked his wife.
  "Well," said the "sage," "if I were the czar, I would do a little
teaching on the side."
A *Treasury of Jewish Humor*, ed. Nathan Ausubel

No person can give a better example of his skill and inclination
than that for the people he is teaching to arrive and live, at the
very least, in a state of their own reason.
BARUCH SPINOZA

Education is that which remains when one has forgotten everything he learned at school.
ALBERT EINSTEIN, *Out of My Later Years*

Curiosity has its own reason for existing. One cannot help but
be in awe when he contemplates the mysteries of eternity, of
life, of the marvelous structure of reality. It is enough if one tries

merely to comprehend a little of this mystery every day. Never lose a holy curiosity.

ALBERT EINSTEIN

My mother made me a scientist without ever intending it. Every other Jewish mother in Brooklyn would ask her child after school: "So? Did you learn anything today?" But not my mother. She always asked me a different question. "Izzy", she would say, "did you ask a good question today?" That difference—asking good questions—made me become a good scientist.

ISIDOR I. RABI, in *The New York Times*, January 19, 1988

I will not close myself off in the house of study when there is no bread in my home.

Ethics of the Fathers 3:17

Creative minds have always been known to survive any kind of bad training.

ANNA FREUD in a speech, 1968

I knew even as a child that the world which we see is not the whole world. Whether you call them demons or angels or some other name, I knew then, and I know today, that there are entities of whom we have no idea and they do exist. You can call them spirits, ghosts, or imps. After all, let's not fool ourselves, a few hundred years ago we didn't know about microbes, we didn't know about electrons and all those powers connected with radiation. So who says that we have already come to the summit of knowledge?

ISAAC BASHEVIS SINGER, *Conversations*

Fill your time to whatever extent you can by learning about things that are divine, not simply to know them but also to do them; and when you shut your book, observe around you, see

within you, to know if by your hand you can make into a deed something that has been learned.
MOSES OF EVREUX

Above all we take pride in the education of our children.
JOSEPHUS

No one has yet fully realized the wealth of sympathy and kindness and generosity hidden in the soul of the child. The effort of every true educator should be to unlock that treasure — to stimulate the child's impulses and call forth the best and noblest tendencies.
EMMA GOLDMAN

Say not, "When I have leisure I will study." Perhaps you will have no leisure.
Ethics of the Fathers 2:3

If one person says, "You're a donkey," don't mind; if two say this, be worried; if three say so, get a saddle.
adapted from MIDRASH RABBAH

Not to answer is an answer.
YIDDISH FOLK SAYING

The most incomprehensible thing about the world is that it is comprehensible.
ALBERT EINSTEIN

To be conscious that you are ignorant is a great step to knowledge.
BENJAMIN DISRAELI

The business of the philosopher is well done if he succeeds in raising genuine doubts.

Morris Raphael Cohen

We should take care not to make the intellect our god; it has, of course, powerful muscles, but no personality.

Albert Einstein

A person's wisdom makes his face shine.

Ecclesiastes 8:1

There are four types of men in this world:
>   The man who knows, and knows that he knows: he is wise, so consult him.
>   The man who knows, but doesn't know that he knows: help him not forget what he knows.
>   The man who knows not, and knows that he knows not: teach him.
>   Finally, there is the man who knows not but pretends that he knows: he is a fool, so avoid him.

Solomon ibn Gabriol, *Choice of Pearls*

Let not a simple parable seem trivial in your eyes, for through it you acquire an insight into the complex law.

Song of Songs Rabbah 1:8

Let your house be a meeting place for the sages, and sit amid the dust at their feet, and drink in their words with thirst.

Ethics of the Fathers 1:4

Imagination is more important than knowledge.

Albert Einstein

This is My covenant with you . . . the words which I have put into your mouth shall not depart from you . . . nor from your children, nor from your children's children henceforth and forever.

ISAIAH 59:21

Wisdom is to the soul as food is to the body.

ABRAHAM IBN EZRA

Approach a goat from the back, a horse from the front, and a stupid man from no direction whatsoever.

YIDDISH FOLK SAYING

Thinking is more precious than all five senses.

NACHMAN OF BRATSLAV

The wise man hears one word—and understands two.

FOLK SAYING

As a Jew, I share a strong commitment to the Jewish intellectual tradition. That tradition places emphasis on learning—learning for the sake of understanding and perfecting our world, and learning for its own sake. Through the ages, we have taken pride in being known as the "People of the Book" and have carried our Torah and our traditions with dignity and affection. Even in the face of persecution and dispersion, and often denied access to centers of learning, the Jewish people, never satisfied with conventional answers, have always valued intellectual inquiry and continued to honor wisdom and learning . . . finally, Judaism represents a great synthesis of universal and Jewish values. For me as a Jew, there need be no conflict between science and religion. Moses Maimonides, philosopher and codifier of Hala-cha (Jewish Law), also graced the world of medicine. He is a role model of living in two worlds, Jewish and universal, and of making them one.

ROSALYN YALOW in *The New York Times*, Sunday, March 7, 1993

Where there is no Torah, there is no proper conduct; where there is no proper conduct, there is no Torah.

Ethics of the Fathers 3:21

For others, a knowledge of the history of their people is a civic duty, while for the Jews it is a sacred duty.

MAURICE SAMUEL, *The Professor and the Fossil*

What the world needs is a fusion of the sciences and the humanities. The humanities express the symbolic, poetic, and prophetic qualities of the human spirit. Without them we would not be conscious of our history; we would lose our aspirations and the graces of expression that move men's hearts. The sciences express the creative urge in man to construct a universe which is comprehensible in terms of the human intellect. Without them, mankind would find itself bewildered in a world of natural forces beyond comprehension, victims of ignorance, superstition and fear.

ISIDOR I. RABI

From the strictly historical point of view the Talmud was never completed . . . The final edition of the Talmud may be compared to the stages of maturity of a living organism; like a tree, it has reached a certain form that is not likely to change substantially, although it continues to live, grow, proliferate. Although the organism has taken on this final form, it still produces new shoots that draw sustenance from the roots and continue to grow . . . [The Talmud] is the collective endeavor of the entire Jewish people. Just as it has no one protagonist, no central figure

who sums up all discussions and subjects, so it has continued throughout the centuries to be part of a constant creative process.
ADIN STEINSALTZ, *The Essential Talmud*

Life is a dream for the wise, a game for the fool, a comedy for the rich, a tragedy for the poor.
SHOLOM ALEICHEM

Men and nations behave wisely once they have exhausted all other alternatives.
ABBA EBAN, December 16, 1970

Foremost among the philosophers of Chelm was a certain Lemach ben Lekish. No question was too deep for him. Take the following as mere illustrations:

"Why," he was asked, "does a dog wag his tail?"

"Because," Lemach answered without hesitation, "the dog is stronger than the tail. Were it the other way, the tail would wag the dog."

Again he was asked why the hair on a man's head turns gray sooner than his beard.

"It's because," Lemach replied, "the hair on his head is twenty years older than his beard."

"And why," he was further asked, "are the waters of the seas salty?"

"Don't you know?" he said. "It's because so many thousands of herring live in them."
A *Treasury of Jewish Folklore*, ed. Nathan Ausubel

Let not the simplest parable seem trivial in thine eyes, for through it thou acquirest an insight into the complex Law.
SONG OF SONGS RABBAH 1:8

A young man from Chelm, who was studying to be a sage, felt very much troubled in mind. So he went to the Chief Sage and asked him, "Perhaps you can tell me why no hair is growing on my chin? Now it could be heredity—or could it? Take my father—you know what a fine thick beard he has."

The Chief Sage reflectively stroked his beard for a while and then his face lit up.

"Perhaps you take after your mother!" he suggested.

"That must be it, since my mother has no beard!" cried the youth with admiration. "What a sage you are!"

A *Treasury of Jewish Folklore*, ed. Nathan Ausubel

"Which is more important, the sun or the moon?" a citizen of Chelm asked his rabbi.

"The moon, of course," replied the rabbi. "It shines at night, when it is needed. The sun shines only during the day, when there is no need of it at all!"

A *Treasury of Jewish Folklore*, ed. Nathan Ausubel

Academic chairs are many, but wise and noble teachers are few.

ALBERT EINSTEIN, *The World as I See It*

Hindsight, usually looked down upon, is probably as valuable as foresight, since it does include a few facts.

GRACE PALEY, "Friends," *Grace Paley: The Collected Stories*

To learn the whole Talmud is a great accomplishment; to learn one virtue is even greater.

YIDDISH FOLK SAYING

The heaven born are the votaries of the arts and of knowledge, the lovers of learning. For the heavenly element in us is the mind, as the heavenly beings are each of them a mind.

PHILO, *On the Giants*

The final aim of knowledge is to hold that we know nothing.
PHILO, *The Migration of Abraham*

The power of thinking has two servants: the power of memory and the power of imagination.
ZOHAR

Languages are spiritual organisms, vital works of art, each of them having its measure of creative power, splendor, depth, logic to explore and to construct the world of nature in life.
NAHMAN SYRKIN

The Hebrew language . . . is the only glue which holds together our scattered bones. It also holds together the rings in the chain of time . . . It binds us to those who built pyramids, to those who shed their blood on the ramparts of Jerusalem, and to those who, at the burning stakes, cried Shema Yisrael!
ISAAC L. PERETZ, *Alle Verk*

About Yiddish: I feel best in this language. I am not self-conscious. In Yiddish, I feel like a man at home—you take off your tie, you take off your jacket—although I don't take off my tie and my jacket at home, but this is my own business.
ISAAC BASHEVIS SINGER, *Conversations*

What is lofty can be said in any language, and what is mean should be said in none.
MAIMONIDES

If a horse with four legs can sometimes stumble, how much more a man with only one tongue.
SHOLOM ALEICHEM

There is first the question of the educated man; and then there is the rather flat fact of which we are all most uncomfortably aware, that our average university graduate emerges from his years of study as something less than an educated man or woman. He is likely to be most strikingly wanting in the accomplishment of perceptivity, in the noncurricular attributes of sensitiveness and of consideration toward all those finer arts which are generally conceded to have played a great part in the humanizing of man.

BEN SHAHN, *Shape and Content*

Mr. Kaplan rose. No other student had risen, but there was something eminently fitting, almost teleological, about Mr. Kaplan's rising. Mr. Pinsky observed every motion of the ascent with the humility of a weaker spirit. A rustle, compact of anticipation, pleasure, and anxiety, went through the classroom.

"Ladies an' gentlemen," Mr. Kaplan began, in his finest oratorical manner.

"Mr. Pockheel told us, a lonk time beck awreddy, dat if ve vant to *loin*, den avery place ve goink, ve should vatchink for mistakes, for Haupen Quastions. In de sopvay, on de stritt, in de alevatits—poblic or private, day an' night, alvays ve shoud be *stoodents!* Believe me, dat vas a fine, smot idea!" Mrs. Moskowitz nodded reverently, as if to a reading of the Psalms. "So like Mr. Pockheel said, avery place I vas goink I vas vatchink, vatchink"— Mr. Kaplan narrowed his eyes and looked suspicious, to lend authenticity to his "vatchink, vatchink"—"all de time vatchink for tings I shoould esk by Haupen Quastions time!"

LEO ROSTEN, *The Education of Hyman Kaplan*

I could not possibly have compiled this book without this well-known wise tale which comforts me every time I have large groups staying with me for a week and then return to my simple quiet

family of six . . . although I always thought there were pigs in the
story . . .

Once a poor Hasid became so distraught because of the crowd-
ing in his hovel that he appealed to his Zaddik for advice.
"Rebbe," he cried, "we have so many children (may no Evil Eye
fall on them!) and so many relatives living with us, that my wife
and I cannot turn around in the house!"

"Have you also a goat?" asked the gitter Yid.

"Why not?" answered the other. "What Jew doesn't own a goat?"

"Then my counsel is that you bring the animal into your
dwelling."

This greatly mystified the Hasid, but he did not dare argue.
The next day, however, having done as he had been told, the
unhappy man came running back to the Zaddik. "Beloved
Rebbe," he groaned, "things now are worse than ever!"

"Have you any chickens?" he was asked.

"What then? How can a Jew live without a few chickens in
his yard?"

"My counsel is that you bring them likewise into your house."

Again the Hasid could not bring himself to argue, but after a
day with the chickens underfoot and on every rafter, he returned
once more to the Zaddik, this time half-crazed.

"So it is bad, eh, my son?" the other said calmly.

"It is the end of the world!" replied the Hasid.

"Very well, then. Now go home, turn out the goat and the
chickens, and come back to me on the morrow."

The following day the Hasid showed up with his face beam-
ing.

"Rebbe!" he cried, "a thousand blessings on thee! My hut
seems like a palace now!"

from A *Treasury of Yiddish Stories*, ed. Irving Howe and
Elize Greenberg

They asked Rabbi Levi Yitzhak: "Why is the first page number missing in all the tractates of the Babylonian Talmud? Why does each begin with the second [the number bet]." He replied: However much a man may learn, he should always remember that he has not even gotten to the first page.

MARTIN BUBER, *Tales of the Hasidim*

More than any other time in history, mankind faces a crossroads. One path leads to despair and utter hopelessness. The other, to total extinction. Let us pray we have the wisdom to choose correctly.

WOODY ALLEN, "To the Graduates," *Side Effects*

WOMEN

Nearly FIVE YEARS AGO, my eldest daughter, Julie, became a bat mitzvah. Traditional Orthodox Judaism provides little guidance for that milestone. So, with the assistance of an Israeli scholar, Gary Shapiro, and my sister Naomi in Israel, I set about to create a service of our own. We selected the stories of nine biblical women, offering their examples, their insights, and their blessings. Sarah's patience, Rebecca's vision, Miriam's music, Ruth's loyalty, Deborah's wisdom, Chanah's faith, and Shulamit's peerless invocation of love are just some of the references we included.

It was our hope that the words offered by her mother, grandmothers, great-grandmother, and aunts—along with Julie's own biblical presentation—would fortify her sense of belonging to the unbroken chorus of Jewish women throughout time who take responsibility for their share in the Torah and the community.

When Nina, our second daughter, celebrated her bat mitzvah three years later, we used the same home-crafted service for her, as have three of my nieces with a few of their own creative additions to the program. With five more female cousins to go, our family considers this a bona fide tradition.

The nature of tradition is that it evolves. Traditions change, some disappear and give rise to new ones based on the social and political climate. Without growth and change, cultures calcify or die. As Jews, we keep some customs that date back to biblical times; other customs followed the destruction of the Temple while still others were instituted in the last few centuries. Hasidism, for example, is only two hundred years old. The traditional role of women in Judaism has also changed considerably over the last fifty years. Although, even in seventeenth- and eighteenth-century Europe, where women played much more classic familial roles, there were women who studied, wrote supplicatory prayers and scholarly works (some included here), and even earned their livelihoods in the marketplace so that their husbands could study.

My family has been fortunate. As I did, my daughters study the Bible, Talmud, and Hebrew literature alongside boys. My mother always worked when we were growing up and her devotion to both the values of a Jewish home and her career left their mark. Women deserve to be heard and to make their own choices in Judaism, something which continues to be problematic in our society. No woman who has chosen a life as a homemaker needs proof of its profound value and impact. Our heritage can be enriched by the voices of all women—those of the rabbi or cantor in a Reform or Conservative synagogue, the women who pray and read from the Torah together in an Orthodox Women's Service, the scholars and the women who simply continue to observe the rituals in their daily lives. Change comes slowly and women's right to participate in Jewish study and ritual at the level they desire it must be recognized.

Included here is only a small sampling of the women who have made their desires clear. Their spiritual gifts and uplifting voices have been discovered and included in excellent anthologies by Dianne Ashton and Ellen Umansky, Sondra Henry and Emily Taitz, and Susannah Heschel. From Beruriah in the Talmud, Gluckel of Hameln in the seventeenth century, to contemporary writers such as Cynthia Ozick, Betty Friedan, Kim Chernin, and Grace Paley, there is continuity in their insights and wisdom. Such contributions will hopefully enable my daughters and granddaughters to more freely express themselves in the collective spiritual enterprise of the Jewish people.

What would happen if one woman told the truth about her life? The world would split open.
MURIEL RUKEYSER

There are those who find this passage from Proverbs condescending to women. I have always felt that it portrays the woman as the strength and center of the family, of which we should never be ashamed.

A woman of valor who can find?
For her price is far above rubies.
The heart of her husband does safely trust in her,
And he has no lack of gain.
She does him good and not evil
All the days of her life . . .
She rises also while it is still night,
And gives food to her household,
And a portion to her maidens.
She considers a field and buys it;
With the fruit of her hands she plants a vineyard.
She girds her loins with strength,
And makes strong her arms . . .
She stretches out her hand to the poor;
Yea, she reaches forth her hand to the needy.
Strength and dignity are her clothing;

And she laughs at the time to come.
She opens her mouth with wisdom;
And the law of kindness is on her tongue.
She looks well to the ways of her household,
And eats not the bread of idleness.
Her children rise up and call her blessed;
Her husband also, and he praises her:
Many daughters have done valiantly,
But you exceed them all.
Grace is deceitful, and beauty is vain;
But a woman that fears the Lord, she shall be praised.
Give her of the fruit of her hands;
And let her works praise her in the gates.
PROVERBS 31:10–31

A woman and a Jew, sometimes more of a contradiction than I can sweat out, yet finally the intersection that is both collision and fusion, stone and seed.
MARGE PIERCY, "The Ram's Horn Sounding," *Available Light*

The Holy One, blessed be He, endowed women with more insight than men.
TALMUD: NIDDAH 45b

My son, heed the discipline of your father, and do not forsake the instruction of your mother.
PROVERBS 1:8

As is the mother, so is the daughter.
EZEKIEL 18:20

Beruriah, the second-century female scholar, was known for her incisive quips:

Once, when R. Yose the Galilean, meeting her along the way, asked, "By which road should we travel in order to reach Lydda?" she replied: "Damn fool! Did not the rabbis say, 'Talk not overmuch with women?' You should have asked: 'How to Lydda?' "

TALMUD: ERUVIN 53b

The Holy One, Blessed be He, said to Moses, "Go speak to the daughters of Israel [and ask them] whether they wish to receive the Torah." Why were the women asked first? Because the way of men is to follow the opinion of women.

PIRKEL D'RABBI ELIEZER 41

God could not be everywhere, so he created mothers.

FOLK SAYING

Cause no woman to weep, for God counts her tears . . . Israel was redeemed because of the virtue of its women.

TALMUD

Rebecca Tiktiner lived in Poland in the sixteenth century and her Meneket Rivka *contains moral teachings, selections from the Talmud and Mishna, and poetry. She was also a translator. In the following prayer she wrote as an introduction to her book, she explains metaphorically why she chose to write her book and how grateful she is for her education.*

I had seen. In my heart I meditated. With my voice I called out. Here, I have now come. And today I walked. And a well of fresh water I found. And I discovered the big stone from the well. And from it I drank. And I was still thirsty. And I said in my heart. I will go and I will bring. To all my near ones. And my bones will rejoice. That they will drink for the length of their days. To fulfill what is said: drink blessed water and you will be blessed by the Blessed. And so with those who are sheltered in Your shade. And so it was promised to us by Your prophets. It will not be removed from the mouths of the seed of your seed. And I also, Your handmaid. The daughter of Your righteous ones. To fulfill Your words. And I shall also come after You. And I fulfilled Your commandments. To follow in Your Torah. Because all of my good, all, is from You. And my resting place is after (in) You. And I will look to Your ways. For Your words are a candle to my feet. In order that You be just in all Your judgments. For You are close to all who call out to You. And to all who desire to see You. They will merit resting in the pleasure of your eyes.

from *Written Out of History*, ed. Sondra Henry and Emily Taitz

Rebbetzin Mizrachi was a learned woman of sixteenth-century Kurdistan, and a teacher in her husband's yeshiva. When she was offered in marriage, her father stipulated that she must never be troubled by housework. When her husband died, she become solely responsible for the administration and maintenance of the school. In Muslim countries, it was not customary for women to walk in the streets let alone run yeshivas.

To whom can I turn?
To the generous people who can cure my ills.
You righteous one, please spare me,
And remember my deeds and the Torah of my God.
Not for my pleasure or my personal benefit am I crying here.
Not for the need of my household, my clothes, or my food.
But only to preserve the Midrashot [biblical explanations]
That my valour will not be shattered . . .

. . . If the students of God will be scattered,
What will become of my world,
Of my days and nights?
Therefore, listen, pious and righteous people . . .

from *Written Out of History*

Rachel Morpurgo was a prolific Italian poet (1790–1871). It is said that in her teens she was already learned in the Talmud, Italian literature, Rashi's commentaries, and the Zohar.

THEN WE'LL BE
PRIVILEGED

We'll be privileged to go out
Chanting and dancing
To sing with a voice so pleasing,
To the Good Shepherd.

The mountains and hills
Will break forth in song.
The tree leaves will clap
Their hands.

To give thanks unto the Lord
In the Temple Ariel
Then the entire nation will see!

Into Zion comes a saviour
The salvation of Israel.
And in their lead, Hananel.

Before her death she wrote:

Alas my wit is weak,
My wound in despair.
See my days draw to the close
I acknowledge my sins.
I return home to God
I serve my Creator
With willing heart,

I thank Him for all He has done
for me.
from *Written Out of History*

On the conflict between domestic responsibility and professional-
ism or creativity, Nina Salaman (1877–1925), an English poet and
translator, wrote this poem.

LOST SONGS

How long the singing voices in my heart
Have all been silent! Day by day the sound
Of noisy nothings whirling through their round.
Of restless nullity has dulled the smart
Which silencing of life's whole truer part
Must cost the soul; and hours and days abound
When not one space for hearkening may be found
And not one stillness for the tears to start.
Only at night, amid the quiet rain,
Or scent of flowers, or in the full moon's sight,
Sometimes a thought comes back, and then the pain
Of some lost poem floating on the night
Brings to the heart its inmost song again,
The weakening whispers of its old delight.
from *Written Out of History*

When therefore the author looks to the support of her own sex
for the support and countenance of her labours . . . she ventures
to hope that from all undue presumption her efforts may be
absolved. Her aim is to aid, not to dictate; to point to the Foun-
tain of Life, not presumptuously to lead; to waken the spirit to
its healing influence, to rouse it to a sense of its own deep responsibilities, not to censure and judge . . .To the mothers and

daughters in Israel its pages are particularly addressed: for to them is more especially entrusted the regeneration of Israel.
GRACE AGUILAR, *Spirit of Judaism*

Women in Israel is considered to be Grace Aguilar's greatest work. In it she defends the role of women in the Jewish tradition:

We have scanned every statute, every law, alike in the words of Moses, and in their simplifying commentary by our elders, and the result of such examination has been, we trust, to convince every woman of Israel of her immortal destiny, her solemn responsibility, and her elevated position, alike by the command of God, and the willing acquiescence of her brother man.

Aguilar wrote a poem about Hagar's predicament:

"What aileth thee, oh Hagar?" thus it spoke: "fear not, for
     God hath heard
The lad's voice where he is, — and thou, trust in thy Maker's
     word!
Awake! Arise! Lift up the lad, and hold him in thine hand —
I will of him a nation make, before Me he shall stand."

It ceased, that voice: and silence now, as strangely soft and
     still
The boundless desert once again, with eloquence would fill;
And strength return'd to Hagar's frame, for God hath oped her
     eyes —
And lo! Amid the arid sands a well of water lies!

She had become a school teacher — a job previously the monopoly of men. She was the first Jewess to become a school teacher in Hungary, and for this she was frowned upon and ostracized by various shocked members of the community. Her example inspired me, led me as a young girl to seek out all kinds

of less sheltered activities, into which I entered with all the ardor
of a cause, and I know I felt very brave and heroine-like myself.
REBECCA KOHUT, describing her unusual mother, 1864

WOMEN SONGS
Kadia Molodowsky

I

The faces of women long dead, of our family,
come back in the night, come in dreams to me saying:
We have kept our blood pure through long generations,
we brought it to you like a sacred wine
from the kosher cellars of our hearts.
And one of them whispers:
I remained deserted, when my two rosy apples
still hung on the tree
and I gritted away the long nights of waking between my
  white teeth.

I will go meet the grandmothers, saying:
Your sighs were the whips that lashed me
and drove my young life to the threshold
to escape from your kosher beds.
But whenever the street grows dark you pursue me —
whenever a shadow falls.

Your whimperings race like the autumn wind past me,
and your words are the silken cord
still binding my thoughts.
My life is a page ripped out of a holy book
and part of the first line is missing.

II

There are such spring-like nights here,
when a blade of grass pushes up through the soil

and the fresh dawn is a green pillow
under the skeletons of a dead horse.
And all the limbs of a woman plead for the ache of birth.
And women come down like sick sheep
by the wells—to heal their bodies,
their faces blackened with year-long thirst for a child's cry.

There are such spring-like nights here
when lightning pierces the black soil with silver knives
and pregnant women approach the white tables of the
    hospital
with quiet steps
and smile at the unborn child
and perhaps at death.

There are such spring-like nights here
when a blade of grass pushes up through the soil.
from A Treasury of Yiddish Poetry, ed. Irving Howe and
Eliezer Greenberg

Full participation in all humanitarian objects is at once the aim
of the women's movement and the meeting-point of all religions.
The Jewish religion makes such demands of character and courage that the majority of Jewish women can find their high vo-
cation anew within their own race and religion, and draw thence
their truest inspiration.
BERTHA PAPPENHEIM, "The Jewish Woman in Religious Life,"
The Jewish Review, January 1913

I am in favor of giving women full rights, but most of my friends
are against it. They argue that the woman would then no longer
be the housewife, the mother of her children, the wife to her
husband—in a word, everything would be destroyed. I do not
agree because a woman is a human being just like a man, and

if women are recognized as human beings, they must be granted all the rights of human beings. *Answer:* Justice can reign among people only when they all have equal rights.

"The Bintel Brief" in *How We Lived*

She was . . . referring to an old discussion about feminism and Judaism. Actually, on the prism of isms, both of those do have to be looked at together once in a while.

GRACE PALEY, "Friends," *Grace Paley: The Collected Stories*

We must not speak of women writers in our century (as we cannot speak of women in any area of recognized human achievement) without speaking also of the invisible, the as-innately-capable: the born to the wrong circumstances—diminished, excluded, foundered, silenced.

TILLIE OLSEN, *Silences*

The Orthodox community encourages a brain drain. Jewish women with fine minds are being wooed by secular society to make their contribution there, while the door to Jewish scholarship remains, in great part, closed.

BLU GREENBERG, *On Women and Judaism*

I was ankle-deep in middle age, wading down the waters of assimilation when I discovered that being Jewish was more than I had ever dreamed. How lucky for me. Now I make the calendar with Jewish cycle of celebrations, my table turns with Seder plate, Challah bread, and honey for the New Year. I've learned the whole story. I learned where Chelm, the town of fools, lies on the map. I can tell you wild tales about Jewish gangsters in Chicago and Jewish soldiers in the Czar's army. I expanded my family. Freud and Einstein are cousins of mine, so are Rashi and Maimonides. Once I knew only about Jewish catastrophe, now I can tell a Jewish joke (not so well) and I have seen Torah pointers, cups for Elijah, and menorahs made of clay . . . Today I frequently argue with a God whose existence I question, but I think that the Jewish people has a purpose, a destiny, a reason for being, perhaps only in the wonder of our plot, the continuing effort to make us shape up, behave decently, look at ourselves with a moral eye. I am no longer a mere particle of genetic material spinning out a single life span. I have a past, present and future among my people. Am I ever surprised.

ANNE ROIPHE, *The New York Times*, September 12, 1993

Women have things in common. We have a common history of misogyny. We have a language different from male language in its images and visions and expressions. We have a religion that centers on the synchronicity of our bodies with the cycles of nature, that has an affinity with all living things, a knowledge of the healing arts, a love of life and a holistic view of the cosmos, an awareness of the waxing and waning of everything in the universe, and the knowledge and vision of an imminent female deity with whom we can identify directly. We are all part of an ecological whole.

BATYA BAUMAN, *On Being a Jewish Feminist*, ed. Susannah Heschel

HER MOTHER

E. M. Broner

Mother, I'm pregnant with a baby girl.
What is she doing?
She is singing.
Why is she singing?
Because she is unafraid.

The truth is that it would be a blinding mistake to think that the issue of Jewish women's access to every branch and parcel of Jewish expression is mainly a question of "discrimination" (which, if that were all, would justify it as feminist issue). No. The point is not that Jewish women want equality as women with men, but as *Jews* with *Jews* — to share Jewish history to the hilt.

CYNTHIA OZICK, "Notes Toward Finding the Right Question" in *On Being a Jewish Feminist*, ed. Susannah Heschel

Cynthia Ozick discusses and criticizes women's exclusion from the creative process:

The nature of the excision is this: a great body of Jewish ethical thinkers, poets, juridical consciences — not merely one generation but many; in short, an entire intellectual and cultural organism — has been deported out of the community of Jewish culture, away from the creative center. Not "deported" in the Nazi sense of being taken away to perish, nor in the sense of being deprived of natural increase, but rather in the sense of isolation, confinement away from the main stage of Jewish communal achievement.

CYNTHIA OZICK, "Notes Toward Finding the Right Question" in *On Being a Jewish Feminist*, ed. Susannah Heschel

Until Jewish women are in the same relation to history and Torah as Jewish men are and have been, we should not allow ourselves ever again to indulge in the phrase "the Jewish genius." What we have had is a Jewish half-genius. That is not enough for the people who choose to hear the Voice of the Lord of History. We have been listening with only half an ear, speaking with only half a tongue, and never understanding that we have made ourselves partly deaf and partly dumb.

CYNTHIA OZICK, "Notes Toward Finding the Right Question" in *On Being a Jewish Feminist*, ed. Susannah Heschel

The time is at hand when the voices of the feminine mystique can no longer drown out the inner voice that is driving women on to become complete.

Betty Friedan, *The Feminine Mystique*

The superior mentality for which the Chelmites were famous was not, it should be noted, confined to the men. The women, too, were distinguished for it, as the following tale illustrates.

A stranger once came to Chelm and put up at the tavern. After eating a hearty meal, he asked the mistress of the inn for his account.

"The bread, the soup, and the dessert come to seven kopeks," said she. "For the roast, another seven kopeks. Altogether eleven kopeks."

"Pardon me," said her guest, "two times seven are fourteen."

For a moment the woman was puzzled, but only for a moment.

"No," said she. "Two times seven are eleven. I was a widow with four children. I married a widower who also had four children, and three more children were born to us. Now each of us has seven children, and altogether we have eleven. Two times seven are eleven."

The stranger paid his account, filled with admiration for the acumen of a mere woman.

from *A Treasury of Jewish Humor*, ed. Nathan Ausubel

RACHEL
Rachel

For her blood runs in my blood
and her voice sings in me.
Rachel, who pastured the flocks of Laban,
Rachel, the mother of the mother.

And that is why the house is narrow for me,
and the city foreign,
for her veil used to flutter
in the desert wind.

And that is why I hold to my way
with such certainty,
for memories are preserved in my feet
ever since, ever since.

4 Rules for Women

1. Don't say "I have nothing to worry about" just because you've already got a husband.
2. If your husband likes gefilte fish, don't shove fried fish down his throat and say: "You dope; you don't know what good is."
3. Don't neglect the cleanliness of your house and clothes just because your nexdoorker does it.
4. If you've been cursed with growths of hair on your throat, cheeks or upper lip . . . don't forget that makes a bad impression. Go immediately to your druggist and for one dollar buy Wonderstone.

The Forward, July 25, 1915, in *How We Lived*, ed. Irving Howe and Kenneth Libo

We sit about the table—four little children and I. Through the hall door comes my mother. She washes at a basin in the far corner of the room and, weary, draws a chair to the meal. Her eyelids are very red. She sits silent . . . We eat. She is tired—too tired to talk. Only the children chatter . . . After the long day in the stogie factory, and after supper and the chores for mother, there was my book—*Lamb's Tales*. Before the kitchen stove, when the house was asleep, I'd throw off my shoes, thaw out the

icy tissues that bit all day long in my consciousness, and lose myself. I read and reread the tales with never-flagging interest ... On our day off much "company" came to our tenement rooms. They stayed late in the evenings, and talked of many things. My mother was the life of these gatherings. She argued, opposed, attacked, defended. When the company wearied of talking, someone would start singing—usually my mother. Her voice was clear and sweet, and every word of her song was heard. Her singing was so heartsome that soon all would be joining in, while she would serve tea in tall glasses.
ROSE PASTOR STOKES in *How We Lived*

It's absolutely incumbent on Jewish women to protest and to withdraw their support from any Jewish organization that doesn't take action against sex and race discrimination.
BETTY FRIEDAN in Anne Stone, "Betty Friedan at 55," *Lilith* 1, no. 1 (1992): 41

To a man everything is permissible, to a woman nothing. A man is king over us and may do his will. When I argue that morality is more demanding on women, my husband gets angry and denies it with all his might. There is no such thing as a man with a bad name, but just let one spot fall upon a woman ... Why?!
from a "Bintel Brief" in *How We Lived*

I hate all this political correctness stuff. I don't think there's one definition of pure feminism. We've got to allow for diversity.
BETTY FRIEDAN in *Hadassah Magazine*, November 1993

I feel about mothers the way I feel about dimples: because I do not have one myself, I notice everyone who does.
    Most people who have a dimple or two take them for granted, unaware of how these endearing parentheses puncture a smile. While I spent months of my childhood going to bed with a

button taped into each cheek trying to imprint nature, my dimpled friends fell asleep unappreciative of their genetic gifts. They did not notice what they had always had.

Most people who have a mother take her for granted in much the same way. They accept or criticize her without remarking on the fact that there is a mother there at all — or how it would feel if there were none. I've never had the luxury of being so blasé. Since I lost my mother when I was quite young, I keep pressing my mother-memories into my mind, like the buttons in my cheeks, hoping to deepen an imprint that time has tried to erase.

She was fifty-three when she died; I was fifteen. I had less time with my mother than I've had with my children. Less time than I've known my closest friends, or many colleagues. The truth is, if you subtract the earliest part of my childhood and the darkest months of her illness, my mother and I really knew one another for a scant ten years. I suppose I should be grateful that so little time has left so much to remember.

LETTY COTTIN POGREBIN, *Deborah, Golda and Me*

Members of Israel's Cabinet once suggested to Golda Meir, then Minister of Labor, that a curfew be imposed on women because of a growing number of assaults taking place on the streets. Mrs. Meir objected: "Men are attacking women, not the other way around. If there is going to be a curfew, let the men be locked up, not the women."

FRANCINE KLAGSBRUN, *Voices of Wisdom*

EVE'S BIRTH
(excerpt)
Kim Chernin

Was I summoned
or did I rise
from my own emergency?

Dreaming of a dark and formless thing
that had no eyes
and fashioned mine.
Remembering:
waters, the disquieting wind,
dark earth and dismembering fire:
A servile arc
that roared disquietude,
wakened from slumber; and breath,
ribbed with mortality.

In biblical times, Jewish leaders were not rabbis, nor cantors, nor sextons, nor directors of education. Each role evolved as the need arose. In biblical times leaders were priests, prophets, and wise persons. In addition, there were female judges, prophets, rulers, and teachers. Women were even, like the rabbi of modern times, professional mourners — skilled in dirges, delivering eulogies in poetic metre . . . The rabbis of today have taken away from women what was theirs by tradition.

The full-time professional rabbi as we know him appeared only recently in Jewish life at the end of the eighteenth-century in Germany when demands of secular education, preaching in the vernacular, and theological inquiry beyond the halakhah (law) became the norm. In perspective, the modern rabbi is a relatively recent institution in Jewish life, the result of development and response to the needs of the Jewish community. And now the Jewish community, in continuing responsiveness to its needs, is considering the woman to serve as rabbi . . .

The Jewish community needs that vast and rich reservoir of Jewish knowledge, expertise, and commitment found in its Jewish women . . . What does the contemporary rabbi do which a woman is not capable of doing? A woman can engage in scholarly pursuits, counsel couples and families, lead in study and prayer . . . But above all—she can be a role model, exemplary in moral and religious conduct, which together with learning is the basic requirement of clergy.

SARAH ROTH LIEBERMAN in Francine Klagsbrun, *Voices of Wisdom*

Whatever Sarah has said to you, listen to her voice.

GENESIS 21:12

WE MOTHERS

Nelly Sachs

We mothers,
we gather seed of desire
from oceanic night,
we are gatherers
of scattered goods.

We mothers,
pacing dreamily
with the constellations,
the floods
of past and future,
leave us alone
with our birth
like an island . . .

We who impel sand to love and bring
a mirroring world to the stars—

We mothers,
who rock in the cradles
the shadowy memories
of creation's day—
the to and fro of each breath
is the melody of our love song.

We mothers
rock into the heart of the world
the melody of peace.

I am becoming still more independent of my parents, young as I am, I face life with more courage than Mummy; my feeling for justice is immovable, and truer than hers. I know what I want, I have a goal, an opinion, I have a religion and love. Let me be myself and then I am satisfied. I know that I'm a woman, a woman with inward strength and plenty of courage.

If God lets me live, I shall attain more than Mummy ever has done, I shall not remain insignificant, I shall work in the world and for mankind!

ANNE FRANK, *The Diary of a Young Girl*, 1944

ART AND CREATIVITY

*F*ROM A TRIBE THAT has wandered the globe for thirty-five hundred years comes all manner of expression. From a people oppressed come words and works of liberation; from despair, meaning; from hopelessness, consolation; and from the vast tableau of human tragedy comes comedy, perhaps our most enduring hallmark.

Judaism's earliest artistic expression was in the written word. The majesty of biblical literature transcends its religious appeal and its themes are timeless and universal. Although its initial voice was rabbinic and its poetry hymnal, it touched on every aspect of the human experience.

The first artisan mentioned in the Bible is Bezalel, son of Uri. Commissioned to build the tabernacle, he was "filled with the spirit of God in wisdom, and in understanding, and in knowledge and in all manner of workmanship — to work in gold, and in silver, and in brass, and in cutting of stone for setting, and in carving of wood." (Exodus 31:1–6)

At the Red Sea, Miriam, the first choreographer, leads the women of Israel in song and dance celebrating the climax of their liberation from Egypt, as it is written, "And Miriam the prophetess, the sister of Aaron, took a timbrel in her hand; and all the women went out after her with timbrels and dances. (Exodus 15:20)

King Saul was told to seek out a harp player to relieve him of the evil spirits. "And it came to pass, when the [evil] spirit from God was upon Saul, that David took the harp, and played with his hand; so Saul found relief, and it was well with him, and the evil spirit departed from him." (1 Samuel 16:23)

Painters, sculptors, dancers, musicians, and authors have followed Bezalel, Miriam, and David and the poets of the Bible. Their art and their music moved our ancestors and continue to enrich all of us communally and personally. Whether it is a haunting wordless melody or "nigun" that might have been sung two hundred years ago by a distant relative from Eastern Europe, a Sephardic version from Turkey, or the stories of Sholom Aleichem, each brings to life a resonant world of long ago.

Marcel Proust wrote, "We feel in one world, we think and name in another. Between the two we can set up a system of references, but we cannot fill the gap." Jewish artists have struggled to bridge this gap. Their thoughts on art, creativity, and the influence of their Judaism on their art are the subjects of this section.

We have 613 commandments. The last one is probably the most important because it includes all the others: Kitvu lakhem et hashirah hazot. "You must write this poetry." To be Jewish means to be a poet. There is poetry in the Jewish existence, and we are commanded to see its poetic dimension. We are to write it down in order to share it with as many people as possible; every Jew is commanded to read the Torah, to write it, and thus to transmit it.

ELIE WIESEL, *Against Silence*

I think that a human being, a real artist, should set for himself the greatest goal. If you set for yourself a small goal you have already failed by the very fact that your goal is so small. Run as far as you can or at least try to. Never get tired. Never fall into despair. If you fall, begin again. This is what life is.
ISAAC BASHEVIS SINGER, *Conversations*

When God uttered the words "Let there be light!" He did not create anything new. What He did was what artists and fathers and mothers do — He took something inside Himself and projected it into the external world, pouring His light into the container of created space.
FREEMA GOTTLIEB, *The Lamp of God*

When the heart is glad, the feet are ready to dance.
FOLK SAYING

I cannot tell you how much I love to play for people. Would you believe it — sometimes when I sit down to practice and there is no one else in the room, I have to stifle an impulse to ring for the elevator man to offer him money to come in and hear me.
ARTUR RUBINSTEIN

Every author should weigh his work to determine whether it has any connection with the "Book of Humanity," namely whether humanity will receive any benefit from it.
NACHMAN OF BRATSLAV

Writing comes more easily if you have something to say.
SHOLEM ASCH

Art is the unceasing effort to compete with the beauty of flowers and never succeeding.
MARC CHAGALL, *My Life*

My pen is my harp and my lyre; my library is my garden and my orchard.
JUDAH HA-LEVI

Not everything that is thought should be expressed, not everything that is expressed verbally should be written, and not everything that is written should be published.
RABBI ISRAEL SALANTER

(And had Reb Salanter lived a century later, he would have continued with . . . "and not everything that is published should become a major motion picture.")

When I sit down to write I have a feeling that I'm talking maybe to millions or maybe to nobody.

• • •

I would not call myself the last Yiddish writer but I am certainly one of the last. It is both a tragedy and a responsibility . . .

I like to write ghost stories and nothing fits a ghost better than a dying language. The deader the language the more alive the ghosts. Ghosts love Yiddish, and as far as I know, they all speak it . . . I am sure that millions of Yiddish-speaking ghosts will rise from their graves one day and their first questions will be, "Is there any new book in Yiddish to read?"
ISAAC BASHEVIS SINGER, *Conversations*

I did not particularly like Moses at first, I suppose, because I was under the complete sway of the Hellenic spirit and could not forgive the Jewish Lawgiver his hatred of all imagery and plastic art. I did not realize that Moses in spite of his enmity for art was, nevertheless, himself a great artist endowed with the artist's true spirit. His art, however, like that of his Egyptian countrymen, was directed to the colossal and indestructible. But he did not, like the Egyptians, mold his masterpieces out of brick and granite, rather did he build human pyramids. He carved human obelisks. He took a poor shepherd tribe and out of it created a people, that even like the pyramids defies the centuries, an eternal, holy people, God's people, that might serve as model to all other peoples, indeed, as the prototype of humanity; he created Israel! . . . The writer of these pages might well be proud that his ancestors belong to the noble house of Israel, that he is a descendant of those martyrs who gave the world a God and an ethic, who struggled and suffered on all the battlefields of ideas.

HEINRICH HEINE, *Confessions*

Which is the right course which a man should choose for himself? All the things which are important to us, which bring us some joy, also bring trouble, but you have to take it as it is . . . One is never happy. If a writer is too happy with his writing, something is wrong with him. A real writer always feels as if he hasn't done enough.

ISAAC BASHEVIS SINGER, *Conversations*

The Talmud is the collective endeavor of the entire Jewish people. Just as it has no one protagonist, no central figure who sums up all discussions and subjects, so it has continued throughout the centuries to be part of a constant creative process.

ADIN STEINSALTZ, *The Essential Talmud*

Music Everywhere

When you walked along the Lower East Side of New York, you heard music coming out of most of the open windows: "one, two, three, four," of little girls practicing the piano; the monotonous wail of the boys on the violin. More often, of course, the Victrola was going full blast. You heard opera, Neapolitan folk songs, cantorial chants, Chauncey Olcott singing, "Ireland Must Be Heaven" or Maggie Cline's recording of "Throw Him Down McCloskey," depending upon the neighborhood you were in.

Music was one of the great joys among the immigrant families.

For all these people of perhaps five or six different nationalities, music was not only the common language but also a common love. And there were many occasions when people who did not speak the same language became friends because they could hum the same tune.

Men made sacrifices for music. In many homes the purchase of a violin for the son was included in the budget along with food, rent, and clothing. And thousands of little girls boasted, "I am taking piano lessons."

In my own home my mother had figured out a good system. She ordered me to hang around the house while my sister Matilda was getting her piano lesson, "and listen to everything the teacher says." One day after my sister's lesson, the teacher called me. "Come here," she said, "let me see what you can do." My mother was embarrassed and offered both an apology and that second fifty cents, but the teacher would have none of it. She said that she had this same two-for-one experience in many other homes, and she seemed happy about the whole thing.

In the midst of poverty along came the settlement house, which not only tried to help the newcomer become a citizen, but also offered free music lessons. Thousands of children learned to play and to love music. It did not matter that they didn't play well; to hear a student play the scales gave many an immigrant father a sense of dignity. Nor did it matter that the talent was meager, as it was in my case. What did matter was that we were cultivating a taste for one of the basic values of our existence.

The New York settlement houses still stand, but their role is perhaps different than what it once was. The neighborhoods are different and so are the people. But music has not changed. The love for it is constant. Free music lessons, perhaps not the greatest gift America gave to the immigrant, certainly was one of the kindest.

HARRY GOLDEN, *You're Entitle'*

Life without music is unthinkable,
Music without life is academic.
That is why my contact with music is a total embrace.

LEONARD BERNSTEIN, *Findings*

A Jewish writer is a Jew who writes — it's a way of making a living. Jews are simply a little more crazy than anyone else, driven by history and tradition . . .

WALLACE MARKFIELD in Israel Shenker, *Coat of Many Colors*

Writing on Jewish themes — serious, trifling, abtruse, down-to-earth — brought challenge and delight. On occasion the subject was an individual, but it could just as well be a whole community; I found myself reviewing millennial traditions but also describing events of such ephemeral frivolity and overpowering insignificance that I wondered if my check would be in the mail that week. Each time I examined a Jewish subject there was something to learn, and every so often I learned it. Sometimes

I managed to communicate the lesson, and—praised be those days—occasionally the amusement proved infectious.

ISRAEL SHENKER, *Coat of Many Colors*

The Jewish novel will live until Jewish writers run out of things to complain about, and I don't think there's any danger of that.

DAN GREENBERG in Israel Shenker, *Coat of Many Colors*

I found a Talmudic scholar in a Jerusalem ghetto, but he didn't want to pose on account of his belief. But he was kind and said, "Come to my home later. I will consult the Bible, and if the Bible tells me I can, I will do it." I came back that night, and the scholar went with closed eyes to the library and opened a Bible. Then opening his eyes, he said, "I can do it." He had seen some words from Genesis. "And they shall dance before my eyes."

ALFRED EISENSTAEDT, *Eisenstaedt on Eisenstaedt*

My style hasn't changed much in all these sixty years. I still use, most of the time, existing light and try not to push people around. I have to be as much a diplomat as a photographer. People often don't take me seriously because I carry so little equipment and make so little fuss. When I married in 1949, my wife asked me, "But where are your real cameras?" I never carried a lot of equipment. My motto has always been, "Keep it simple."

ALFRED EISENSTAEDT, *Eisenstaedt on Eisenstaedt*

The artist must penetrate into the world, feel the fate of human beings, of peoples, with real love. There is no art for art's sake. One must be interested in the entire realm of life.

MARC CHAGALL, *Jewish Spectator*, September 1951

I try to choose my readers, and, in so doing, I try not to set my sights too low. I aim at a reader who is intelligent, educated and has good exacting taste. Generally speaking, I feel that a short story can be read properly only by a very intelligent woman—the better specimens of this half of the human race sometimes have absolute taste, just as some people have absolute pitch. The most important thing here is to form a picture of one's reader—a picture as strict as possible. That's how it is with me. My reader lives in my soul, but since he's been there quite a long time, I have fashioned him in my own image. Perhaps he's even become one with me.

ISAAC BABEL, *You Must Know Everything Stories*

A book, like a child, needs time to be born. Books written quickly—within a few weeks—make me suspicious of the author. A respectable woman does not bring a child into the world before the ninth month.

HEINRICH HEINE, *Thoughts and Fancies*

By the time a writer discovers he has no talent for literature, he is too successful to give it up.

GEORGE S. KAUFMAN

The most beautiful thing we can experience is the mysterious. It is the source of all true art and science.

ALBERT EINSTEIN, *What I Believe*

Praise Him with the blast of the horn;
Praise Him with the psaltery and harp;
Praise Him with the timbrel and dance;
Praise Him with the loud-sounding cymbals;
Let every thing that hath breath praise the Lord.
Hallelujah.

PSALM 150

It is this quality of being in love with our subject that is indispensable for writing good history—or good anything for that matter.

BARBARA TUCHMAN in Elinor and Robert Slater, *Great Jewish Women*

This determination of self-criticism may make clear why it is that a number of the most excellent jokes . . . should have sprung into existence from the soil of Jewish national life . . . I do not know whether one often finds a people that makes so merry unreservedly over its own shortcomings.

SIGMUND FREUD, "Wit and Its Relation to the Unconscious"

The funny bone is universal . . . With me humor comes unexpectedly, usually in defense of a character, sometimes because I need cheering up. When something starts funny I can feel my imagination eating and running . . . Comedy, I imagine, is harder to do consistently than tragedy, but I like it spiced in the wine of sadness.

BERNARD MALAMUD interview in *Writers at Work*, ed. George Plimpton

God's dream is . . . to have mankind as a partner in the drama of continuous creation.

ABRAHAM HESCHEL, *Who Is Man?*

It can be said truthfully that art (or the creative act) begins in love and giving, for there must always be present this empathy, this basic act of giving over.

CLIFFORD ODETS, *Clifford Odets, American Playwright . . .*

Look at Jewish history. Unrelieved lamenting would be intolerable. So, for every 10 Jews beating their breasts, God designated one to be crazy and amuse the breast-beaters. By the time I was five I knew I was that one.

MEL BROOKS in "The Mad Mad Mel Brooks," *Newsweek*, February 17, 1975

Why Write a Book?

Rabbi Mendel's hasidim asked him why he did not write a book. For a while he was silent, then he answered, "Well, let's say I have written a book. Now who is going to buy it? Our own people will buy it. But when do our people get to read a book, since all through the week they are absorbed in earning their livelihood? They will get to read it on a sabbath. And when will they get to it on a sabbath? First they have to take the ritual bath, then they must learn and pray, and then comes the sabbath meal. But after the sabbath meal is over, they have time to read. Well, suppose one of them stretches out on the sofa, takes the book, and opens it. But he is full, he feels drowsy, so he falls asleep and the book slips to the floor. Now tell me, why should I write a book?"

MARTIN BUBER, *Tales of the Hasidim*

Writing and the creative process, like all artistic work, are the revelations of a vision which is embodied, knowingly or unknowingly, in every action performed by man and that pulsates in him in every field of life he deals with, with all his heart and being.

CHAIM NACHMAN BIALIK in Mordecai Ovadyahu, *Bialik Speaks*

The principal mark of genius is not perfection but originality, the opening of new frontiers.

ARTHUR KOESTLER

Music can name the unnamable and communicate the un-
knowable.
LEONARD BERNSTEIN, "The Unanswered Question"

To sit in a room alone for six or seven or ten hours, sharing the
time with characters that you created, is sheer heaven.
NEIL SIMON, *Rewrites*

The progression of a painter's work, as it travels in time from
point to point, will be toward clarity: toward the elimination of
all obstacles between the painter and the idea and between the
idea and the observer.
MARK ROTHKO, "Statement on His Attitude in Painting," *The Tiger's
Eye* 9 (October 1949)

I would do better if I lived more healthily, exercised more, ate
less. I'm a hog. I love food and drink. I love tastes and textures.
I think I could be called a sensualist. But that is the power source
of my playing. When I'm caressing music, it is very sensual. I
love feelings and I love gratifying the senses. I would find it
difficult to be abstemious.
ISAAC STERN in *The New Yorker*, June 5, 1965

Playing the violin must be like making love—all or nothing.
ISAAC STERN in *The New Yorker*, June 5, 1965

I feel that art has something to do with the achievement of
stillness in the midst of chaos. A stillness which characterizes
prayer, too, and the eye of the storm. I think that art has something to do with an arrest of attention in the midst of distractions.
SAUL BELLOW in *Writers at Work*, ed. George Plimpton

At every concert, I leave a lot to the moment. I must have the
unexpected, the unforeseen. I want to risk, to dare. I want to be

surprised by what comes out. I want to enjoy it more than the audience. That way the music can bloom anew.
ARNOLD SCHOENBERG in *Great Jews in Performing Arts*

If a composer does not write from the heart, he simply cannot produce good music. I never had a theory in my life. I get a musical idea for a composition, I try to develop a certain logical and beautiful conception and I try to clothe it in music which exudes from it naturally and inevitably. I write what I feel in my heart and what finally comes on the paper is what first coursed through every fiber of my body.
ARNOLD SCHOENBERG in *Great Jews in Performing Arts*

Popular music is popular because a lot of people like it.
IRVING BERLIN

Man plans, God laughs. I have always been a kind of fatalist. I firmly believe that what's going to happen to any of us is already written down in a great big book. Someone up there looked down one day, pointed a long finger at me, and said: That one is going to be a singer with very high notes. I like that notion.
BEVERLY SILLS, *Bubbles*

MY SONG
Chaim Nachman Bialik

Do you know where I got my song?

In my father's house a lonely singer lived,
modest, unobtrusive, diffident,
a dweller in dark crannies, screened in chinks.
He knew one melody, familiar, fixed,
and when my heart grew dumb, and my tongue clove
to the roof of my mouth in silent misery

and stifled weeping welled up in my throat,
into my desolate spirit crept the song
of a chirping cricket, poet of poverty.

The subconscious may greatly shape one's art; undoubtedly it does so. But the subconscious cannot create art. The very act of making a painting is an intending one; thus to intend and at the same time relinquish intention is a hopeless contradiction, albeit one that is exhibited on every hand.
BEN SHAHN, *The Shape of Content*

It is life itself as it chances to exist that furnishes the stimulus for art. That is not to say any special branch or section of life. Any living situation in which an artist finds material pertinent to his own temper is a proper situation for art.
BEN SHAHN, *The Shape of Content*

Form is formulation — the turning of content into a material entity, rendering a content accessible to others, giving it permanence, willing it to the race. Form is as varied as are the accidental meetings of nature. Form in art is as varied as idea itself.
It is the visible shape of all man's growth; it is the living picture of his tribe at its most primitive, and of his civilization at its most sophisticated state. Form is the many faces of the legend — bardic, epic, sculptural, musical, pictorial, architectural; it is the infinite images of religion; it is the expression and the remnant of self. Form is the very shape of content.
BEN SHAHN, *The Shape of Content*

The only way to understand any character is through yourself. Everyone is much more alike than they willingly admit. Even as frantic and fantastic a creature as Blanche is created by things

you have felt and known if you'll dig for them and be honest about what you see.
ELIA KAZAN

I've never tried to plot out my plays to the end, since I've found it as much an exercise in futility as trying to predict what would happen in my own life a month hence. They both invariably unfold and reveal themselves when the appropriate time comes. Suddenly, 5 or 3 or 2 pages before my now expected conclusion, much to my surprise, I would stop writing. Things would appear crystal clear on the paper. The play was done. Everything I wanted to say had just been said. It was finished. All that remained to do was type in the word "Curtain," and turn off the IBM and the lamp over my desk.
NEIL SIMON, *Rewrites*

To approach all music in the vain hope that it will soothe one in the lush harmonies of the late nineteenth century is a common error of many present day music lovers.
AARON COPLAND, *Composers on Music*, ed. Aaron Copland

Music is in a continual state of becoming.
AARON COPLAND

You know, McCarthy is dust and this play is still alive! It's the revenge of art!
ARTHUR MILLER discussing the film version of *The Crucible* in
Entertainment Weekly, December 6, 1996

I believe that when a play questions, even threatens, our social arrangement, that is when it really shakes us profoundly and dangerously, and that is when you've got to be great; good isn't enough.
ARTHUR MILLER in *Writers at Work*, ed. George Plimpton

Being a playwright was always the maximum idea. I'd always felt that the theater was the most exciting and the most demanding form one could try to master. When I began to write, one assumed inevitably that one was in the mainstream that began with Aeschylus and went through about twenty-five hundred years of playwriting. There are so few masterpieces in the theater, as opposed to the other arts, that one can pretty well encompass all of them by the age of nineteen. Today, I don't think playwrights care about history. I think they feel it has no relevance.

ARTHUR MILLER IN *Writers at Work*, ed. George Plimpton

My music has nothing to do with the violin. It's what you have in your head, in your *personality*. When you play music what you're really exploring is yourself.

ITZHAK PERLMAN

I'm trying to write dramatic poetry . . . I'm trying to capture primarily through the rhythm and secondarily through the connotation of the word the intention of the character. So when that is successful, what one ends up with is a play in free verse. If people want to say that it sounds just like people on the bus, that's fine with me, because that's how the people on the bus sound to me.

DAVID MAMET in "David Mamet: Language as Dramatic Action," B.B.C. Radio, 19 April 1985

I try to see the Jew as universal man. Every man is a Jew though he may not know it. The Jewish drama is prototypic, a symbol of the fight for existence in the highest possible human terms. Jewish history is God's gift of drama.

BERNARD MALAMUD, *Conversations*

However glorious the history of art, the history of artists is quite another matter. And in any well-ordered household the very thought that one of the young may turn out to be an artist can be a cause for general alarm. It may be a point of great pride to have a Van Gogh on the living room wall, but the prospect of having Van Gogh himself in the living room would put a good many devoted art lovers to rout.

BEN SHAHN, *The Shape of Content*

Look at those statues. Come closer and see the light streaming from their marble eyes. See how much goodness lies hidden in their stone faces. You call it idolatry, but I tell you that, quite literally, I could weep when I walk about Paris and see these sculptures. It's a miracle, after all. How could a human being breathe the breath of life into stone? When you see a living man, you only see one man. But when you see a man poured out in bronze, you see mankind itself.

CHAIM GRADE, *My Quarrel with Hersh Rassayner*

There are halls in heaven that open only to the voice of song.

ZOHAR

GLOSSARY OF NAMES

ABRAMOWITSCH, S. Y. (Mendele Mocher Sforim) (1834–1917) Belorussian–born Hebrew-Yiddish author
ACHAD HA'AM (Asher Ginzberg) (1856–1927) Russian-born Hebrew essayist, Zionist, and philosopher.
ADLER, MORRIS (1906–1966) Russian-born rabbi in Michigan
AGNON, S. J. (1888–1970) Galician-born Hebrew novelist, Nobel prize winner
AGUILAR, GRACE (1816–1847) English author, poet, and historian
ALEICHEM, SHOLOM (1859–1916) Ukrainian-born Yiddish author and humorist
ALLEN, WOODY Contemporary American writer and filmmaker
ALTERMAN, NATAN (1916–1970) American-Israeli poet
AMICHAI, YEHUDAH Contemporary Israeli poet
ARENDT, HANNAH (1906–1975) German philosopher and writer
ASCH, SHOLEM (1880–1957) Yiddish novelist and playwright
BAAL SHEM TOV (ca. 1700–1760) Ukrainian-born founder of Hasidism
BABEL, ISAAC (1894–1941) Russian author
BAECK, LEO (1873–1956) German rabbi, writer, and philosopher
BAUMAN, BATYA Contemporary American writer and editor
BELLOW, SAUL Contemporary American novelist, Nobel prize winner
BEN-GURION, DAVID (1886–1973) first Israeli prime minister
BEN SIRA (second century B.C.E.) sage and author
BERLIN, IRVING (1888–1989) Russian-born American composer
BERNSTEIN, LEONARD (1918–1990) American composer and conductor
BERURIAH (second century) Talmud scholar
BIALIK, CHAIM NACHMAN (1873–1934) Polish-born Hebrew poet, storyteller, and essayist
BLANKFORT, MICHAEL (1907–1982) American author and playwright
BRICKMAN, MARSHALL Contemporary American writer and filmmaker
BRONER, E. M. Contemporary American writer
BROOKS, MEL Contemporary American filmmaker and actor

BRUCE, LENNY (1925–1966) American comedian and satirist

BUBER, MARTIN (1878–1965) German theologian and author

CHAFETZ CHAIM (Israel Meir Kagan) (1835–1933) Polish rabbi and scholar

CHAGALL, MARC (1887–1985) Russian-born artist

CHAYEFSKY, PADDY Contemporary American screenwriter and playwright

CHERNIN, KIM Contemporary American author and poet

COPLAND, AARON (1900–1990) American composer

CUNNINGHAM, LAURA Contemporary American author

DAYAN, MOSHE (1915–1981) Israeli politician and military leader

DISRAELI, BENJAMIN (1804–1881) British prime minister and novelist

EBAN, ABBA Contemporary Israeli statesman, diplomat, and writer

EINSTEIN, ALBERT (1879–1955) German-born American physicist, Nobel prize winner

EISENSTAEDT, ALFRED (1898–1995) German photojournalist

ELIACH, YAFFA Contemporary Polish-born teacher and writer

FEIFFER, JULES Contemporary American social cartoonist, playwright, and humorist

FERBER, EDNA (1887–1968) American novelist

FEYNMAN, RICHARD (1918–1988) American physicist, writer, Nobel prize winner

FRANK, ANNE (1929–1945) Holocaust victim and diarist

FRANKFURTER, FELIX (1882–1965) United States Supreme Court justice

FREUD, ANNA (1895–1982) Austrian-born child psychologist

FREUD, SIGMUND (1856–1939) Austrian-born psychoanalyst

FRIEDAN, BETTY Contemporary American feminist leader and author

FRIEDLANDER, ISRAEL (1877–1922) American Orientalist

GINSBERG, ALLEN (1926–1997) American poet and activist

GLUCKEL OF HAMELN (1645–1724) Yiddish author

GOLDBERG, LEAH (1911–1970) Lithuanian-born Hebrew and Russian poet

GOLDEN, HARRY (1902–1981) American newspaper publisher and author

GOLDMAN, EMMA (1869–1940) Lithuanian-born anarchist and author

GOLDMAN, SOLOMON (1893–1953) American rabbi, scholar, and author

GOLDSTEIN, ISRAEL (1896–1986) American rabbi, Zionist leader, and author

GOLDSTEIN, REBECCA Contemporary American writer

GORDON, A. D. (1856–1922) Russian-born Hebrew writer and Zionist philosopher

GRADE, CHAIM (1910–1982) Lithuanian-born Yiddish novelist and poet

GRAUBART, JUDY Contemporary American actress and writer

GREENBERG, BLU Contemporary American writer and feminist spokesperson

GREENBERG, DANIEL Contemporary American journalist

HALEVI, JUDAH (1075–1141) poet and philosopher

HEINE, HEINRICH (1797–1856) German lyric poet and novelist

HELLMAN, LILLIAN (1906–1984) American playwright

HERZL, THEODOR (1860–1904) Viennese journalist and father of political Zionism

HESCHEL, ABRAHAM JOSHUA (1907–1972) American rabbi, philosopher, author, and activist

HIRSCH, SAMSON RAPHAEL (1808–1888) German rabbi, scholar, and author

IBN EZRA, ABRAHAM (1089–1164) Spanish scholar and poet

IBN GABRIOL, SOLOMON (c. 1021–1056) Spanish philosopher and poet

IBN ZABARA (fourteenth century) Spanish author and poet

IMBER, N. H. (1856–1909) Hebrew poet

JOSEPH, MORRIS (1848–1930) British theologian

JOSEPHUS (first century) Jewish historian and general

KAPLAN, MORDECHAI M. (1881–1983) American rabbi and founder of the reconstructionist movement

KAUFMAN, GEORGE S. (1889–1961) American playwright and stage director

KAZAN, ELIA Contemporary Turkish-born American film director

KAZIN, ALFRED Contemporary American author, critic, and editor

KLAGSBRUN, FRANCINE Contemporary American author and social activist

KOESTLER, ARTHUR (1905–1983) British author

KOZOL, JONATHAN Contemporary American writer

KUSHNER, HAROLD Contemporary American rabbi and author

LAZARUS, EMMA (1849–1887) American poet

LEBOW, FRED (1932–1994) Father of the New York City marathon

LERMAN, RHODA Contemporary American author

LESTER, JULIUS Contemporary American author and professor

LEVANT, OSCAR (1906–1972) American author, actor, and musician

LEVENSON, SAM (1914–1980) American comedian and writer

LEVI, PRIMO (1919–1987) Italian author, poet, chemist, and Holocaust survivor

LEWISOHN, LUDWIG (1882–1955) American novelist and editor

LIEBERMAN, SARAH ROTH Contemporary American educator

LOOKSTEIN, HASKEL Contemporary American Orthodox rabbi, educator, and author

LOOKSTEIN, JOSEPH (1903–1979) American Orthodox rabbi, educator, and author

LUZZATTO, MOSES HAYYIM (1707–1747) Italian poet and mystic

LUZZATTO, SAMUEL DAVID (1800–1865) Italian scholar and philosopher

MAIMONIDES, MOSES (1135–1204) Spanish scholar, philosopher, and physician

MALAMUD, BERNARD (1914–1986) American writer

MAMET, DAVID Contemporary playwright, screenwriter, and essayist

MARKFIELD, WALLACE Contemporary American writer

MARX, GROUCHO (1895–1977) American comedian, actor, and writer

MEIR, GOLDA (1898–1978) Israeli prime minister

MILLER, ARTHUR Contemporary American playwright, novelist, and essayist

MILLU, LIANNA Contemporary Italian journalist, author, and Holocaust survivor

MOISE, PENINA (1797–1880) American poet and teacher

MOLODOWSKY, KADIA (1894–1975) Polish-born Yiddish poet and novelist

MORPURGO, RACHEL (1790–1871) Italian Hebrew poet

MOSES OF EVREUX (thirteenth century) French scholar

NACHMAN OF BRATSLAV (1772–1810) Hasidic rabbi and leader

NADICH, HADASSAH Contemporary culinary expert

NADIR, MOSHE (1885–1943) Yiddish poet and humorist

ODETS, CLIFFORD (1906–1963) American playwright and screenwriter

OPPENHEIMER, J. ROBERT (1904–1967) American nuclear physicist

OZICK, CYNTHIA Contemporary American author, playwright, essayist, and social philosopher

PALEY, GRACE Contemporary American author

PAPPENHEIM, BERTHA (1859–1936) Austrian-born German feminist leader and writer

PERELMAN, S. J. (1904–1979) humorist and screenwriter

PERETZ, ISAAC L. (1852–1915) Polish-born Yiddish novelist, poet, and critic

PERL, GISELLA (d. 1985) Hungarian-born writer and Holocaust survivor

PHILO (first century) Alexandrian philosopher, biblical scholar, and author

PIERCY, MARGE Contemporary American author

POGREBIN, LETTY COTTIN Contemporary American author and feminist

PROUST, MARCEL (1871–1922) French novelist

RABI, ISIDOR I. (1898–1988) Austro-Hungarian–born American physicist, Nobel prize winner

RABIN, YITZHAK (1922–1995) Israeli prime minister

RAPOPORT, NESSA Contemporary American author and editor

RASHI (1040–1105) French writer and biblical and Talmudic commentator

REZNIKOFF, CHARLES (1894–1976) American author and poet

RODEN, CLAUDIA Contemporary cookbook author

ROIPHE, ANNE Contemporary American writer

ROSTEN, LEO (1907–1997) American author and humorist

ROTHCHILD, SYLVIA Contemporary American writer

ROTHKO, MARK (1903–1970) Russian-born artist

RUBENSTEIN, ARTUR (1886–1982) Polish-born piano virtuoso

RUKEYSER, MURIEL (1913–1980) American poet and author

SACHS, NELLY (1891–1970) German-born poet and Holocaust survivor

SALANTER, RABBI ISRAEL LIPKIN (1810–1883) Lithuanian rabbi and moralist

SAMUEL, MAURICE (1895–1972) Romanian-born essayist and novelist

SCHECHTER, SOLOMON (1847–1915) Romanian-born scholar, author, and educator

SCHOENBERG, ARNOLD (1874–1951) Austrian-born composer

SCHWARTZ, DELMORE (1913–1966) American poet, author, and critic

SCHWARTZ, LYNNE SHARON Contemporary American novelist, essayist, and translator

SENESH, HANNAH (1921–1944) Hungarian-born Israeli poet and activist

SHAHN, BEN (1898–1969) Lithuanian-born artist and author

SHENKER, ISRAEL Contemporary American journalist and author

SHOSTECK, PATTI Contemporary American author
SILLS, BEVERLY Contemporary American opera singer
SILVERSTEIN, RABBI BARUCH (1914–1995) Polish-born rabbi and author
SILVERSTEIN, EDITH Contemporary American culinary artist
SIMON, KATE Contemporary American writer
SIMON, NEIL Contemporary American playwright
SINGER, ISAAC BASHEVIS (1904–1991) Polish-born novelist, Nobel prize winner
SPINOZA, BARUCH (1632–1677) Dutch philosopher and author
STEINBERG, MILTON (1903–1950) American rabbi, author, and scholar
STEINSALTZ, ADIN Contemporary Israeli rabbi, Talmudic scholar, and author
STERN, ISAAC Contemporary American violinist
STOKES, ROSE PASTOR (1879–1933) Polish-born socialist writer and lecturer
SYRKIN, NAHMAN (1868–1924) Belorussian-born Socialist Zionist leader and author
SZOLD, HENRIETTA (1860–1945) American Zionist and philanthropist
TCHERNICHOVSKY, SAUL (1875–1943) Russian-born Hebrew poet
TIKTINER, REBECCA (c. 1520–1550) Czech writer and translator
TUCHMAN, BARBARA (1912–1989) American journalist, author, historian, Pulitzer prize winner
USSISHKIN, MANAHEM (1863–1943) Russian-born Zionist leader and writer
VIORST, JUDITH Contemporary American writer
WEIL, SIMONE (1909–1943) French philosopher and author
WEIZMANN, CHAIM (1874–1952) Russian-born chemist, Zionist leader, and the first president of Israel
WIESEL, ELIE Contemporary Romanian-born author, professor, and leading spokesperson on the Holocaust
WOLF, FRAU FRUMET (c. 1800–1849) Hungarian writer
WOLPE, DAVID Contemporary American rabbi, author, and educator
WOUK, HERMAN Contemporary American author
YALOW, ROSALYN Contemporary American physicist
YEZIERSKA, ANZIA (1885–1970) Russian-born American novelist

GLOSSARY OF ANCIENT SOURCES

(For a more detailed explanation of each of these important Jewish texts, see Joseph Telushkin's Jewish Literacy: The Most Important Things to Know About the Jewish Religion, Its People, and Its History.*)*

Hebrew Bible Refers to the Five Books of Moses (Torah) — Genesis, Exodus, Leviticus, Numbers, and Deuteronomy. These are followed by The Prophets, Psalms, and The Five Megillot (Scrolls).

Mishna A six-volume codification of the Oral Law, based on biblical passages, recorded by Judah HaNasi in 200 B.C.E. They were the end result of four to six centuries of analysis and teaching in Palestine and are divided into sixty-three tractates.

Ethics of the Fathers The only nonlegal tractate of the Mishna, included toward the end of the fourth volume or "order," *Nezikin*. It is a short, extremely accessible book filled with scholars' practical insights, and moral advice as well as spiritual sayings. Jewish tradition encourages the study of one chapter of *Ethics of the Fathers* each Sabbath afternoon in the spring and summer months.

Avot de Rabbi Nathan *(Fathers According to Rabbi Nathan)* Considered one of the minor tractates of the Talmud providing commentary on the *Ethics of the Fathers*.

Talmud Usually refers to the Babylonian Talmud, produced about the year 500. There is also, however, the Jerusalem (sometimes referred to as the Palestine) Talmud, compiled one hundred years before the Babylonian. The Babylonian Talmud, written in Aramaic and Hebrew, follows the organization of orders and tractates in the Mishna but covers much more territory and is much more universal in scope. It is a monumental work containing all the commentaries and discussions of the rabbis or *Amora'im* ("interpreters") on issues of ceremonial and ritual law, ethical principles, science, medicine, magic and folklore, sex, marriage, and child rearing, business and community matters. As a rule, a Talmudic text will begin with a simple passage of the Mishna and then is followed by lengthy discussion, deliberation, and analysis until a final judgment is made.

Midrash Rabbah A compilation of the rabbis' comments on each of the five books of the Torah as well as the Five Scrolls (The Song of Songs, Ruth, Lamentations, Ecclesiastes, and Esther). The Midrash Rabbah is concerned with the *aggadic* (nonlegal) aspects of these works. Parts were compiled in the fifth and sixth centuries; others, during the eighth and tenth centuries.

Mechilta A *midrashic* interpretation on the book of Exodus, written in the first century.

Tanhuma A collection of homilies on the Torah by Rabbi Tanhuma bar Abba, a fourth-century Palestinian scholar, who wrote many *midrashim.*

Zohar The most famous work of kabbalah, written in Aramaic in the thirteenth century by the Spanish rabbi, Moses de Leon, but sometimes attributed to Simon bar Yochai, who lived nearly a thousand years before. The Zohar is written in the form of a commentary on the Torah, weaving together mystical insights with anecdotes about the great sages of Israel.

Mishneh Torah A systematic code of all Jewish law written in the twelfth century by the Spanish philosopher and scholar, Moses Maimonides. It is divided into fourteen volumes and provides commentary on the Torah's 613 commandments.

Guide of the Perplexed This was Moses Maimonides' last major work of Jewish scholarship. In this book, Maimonides offers a philosophic rationale for the Torah's laws.

Apocrypha The books of the Apocrypha were not included in the Bible. Written after Ezra, the great sage of the fifth century B.C.E., the most famous volumes are the books of *Maccabees* and *Ecclesiasticus*, the latter alternatively known as the *Wisdom of Ben Sira*.

SELECTED BIBLIOGRAPHY

Abrahamson, Irving, ed. *Against Silence: The Voice and Vision of Elie Wiesel.* New York: Holocaust Library, 1985.

Abramovitsh, S. Y. *Tales of Mendele the Book Peddler: Fishke the Lame and Benjamin the Third.* New York: Schocken Books, 1996.

Achad Ha'am (Asher Ginsberg). *Essays, Letters, Memoirs.* Translated from the Hebrew and edited by Leon Simon. Oxford: East and West Library, 1946.

Agnon, S. J. *The Bridal Canopy.* Translated by I. M. Lask. Garden City, N.Y.: Doubleday, Doran & Co., 1937.

Aleichem, Sholom. *Stories and Satires by Sholom Aleichem.* Translated by Curt Leviant. New York: Thomas Yoseloff, 1959.

Allen, Woody. *Side Effects.* New York: Random House, Inc., 1980.

Ashton, Dianne, and Ellen M. Umansky, eds. *Four Centuries of Jewish Women's Spirituality—A Sourcebook.* Boston: Beacon Press, 1992.

Ausubel, Nathan. *A Treasury of Jewish Folklore.* New York: Crown Publishers, Inc., 1948.

——, ed. *A Treasury of Jewish Humor.* Garden City, N.Y.: Doubleday & Co., Inc., 1951.

Babel, Isaac. *The Collected Stories of Isaac Babel.* New York: Penguin Group, 1955.

Baron, Joseph. *A Treasury of Jewish Quotations.* Northvale, N.J.: Jason Aaronson Inc., 1985.

Bellow, Saul, ed. *Great Jewish Short Stories.* New York: Laurel Books, 1963.

Ben Shea, Noah. *The Word: A Spiritual Sourcebook.* New York: Villard, 1995.

Bialik, Chaim Nahman, and Yehoshua Hana Ravnitzky, eds. *The Book of Legends, Sefer Ha-Aggadah: Legends from the Talmud and Midrash.* Translated by William G. Braude. New York: Schocken Books, 1992.

Buber, Martin. *Tales of the Hasidim.* New York: Schocken Books, 1975.

Carmi, T., ed. *The Penguin Book of Hebrew Verse*. Philadelphia: Penguin Books, 1981.

Cunningham, Laura. *Sleeping Arrangements*. New York: Penguin Books, 1989.

Efros, Israel, ed. *The Complete Poetic Works of Hayyiam Nahmn Bialik*. New York: The Histadruth Ivrith of America, Inc., 1948.

Eliach, Yaffa. *Hasidic Tales of the Holocaust*. New York: Oxford University Press, 1982.

Farrell, Grace, ed. *Isaac Bashevis Singer: Conversations*. Jackson/London: University Press of Mississippi, 1992.

Frank, Anne. *The Diary of a Young Girl*. Garden City, N.Y.: Doubleday Co., Inc., 1952.

Freedman, Rabbi Dr. H., and Maurice Simon, trans. *Mishna Rabbah*. 5 vols. London: The Soncino Press, Ltd., 1948.

Ginsberg, Allen. *Kaddish and Other Poems from 1958–1960*. San Francisco: City Lights Books, 1961.

Gluckel of Hameln. *The Memoirs of Gluckel of Hameln*. Translated by Marvin Lowenthal. New York: Schocken Books, 1977.

Golden, Harry. *You're Entitle'*. Cleveland, New York: World Publishing Co., 1962.

Goldstein, Rebecca. *The Mind-Body Problem*. New York: Penguin Books, 1993.

Goodhill, Ruth Marcus, ed. *The Wisdom of Heschel*. New York: Farrar, Straus & Giroux, 1975.

Goodman, Philip. *Rejoice in Thy Festival*. New York: Bloch Publishing, 1956.

———. *Holiday Anthologies, Hannukah, Passover, Purim, Sukkot*. Philadelphia: Jewish Publication Society, 1974.

Goodman, Philip, and Hanna Goodman. *The Jewish Marriage Anthology*. Philadelphia: The Jewish Publication Society, 1965.

Greenberg, Sidney, ed. *A Modern Treasury of Jewish Thoughts*. New York/London: Thomas Yoseloff, 1960.

Gross, Theodore L., ed. *The Literature of American Jews*. New York: Free Press, 1973.

Henry, Sondra, and Emily Taitz. *Written Out of History: Our Jewish Foremothers*. New York: Biblio Press, 1990.

Hertz, J. *Pirke Aboth: Sayings of the Fathers*. New York: Behrman House, 1945

Heschel, Abraham Joshua. *The Sabbath*. New York: Farrar, Straus, 1951.

———. *Between God and Man*. New York: The Free Press, 1959.

———. *God in Search of Man*. New York: Meridian Books, Inc., 1959.

———. *The Insecurity of Freedom*. New York: Farrar, Straus, 1966.

Heschel, Susannah, ed. *On Being a Jewish Feminist: A Reader*. New York: Schocken Books, 1983.

Hodes, Aubrey. *Martin Buber, An Intimate Portrait*. New York: Viking Press, 1971.

Howe, Irving, and Eliezer Greenberg, eds. *A Treasury of Yiddish Stories*. New York: Penguin Books, 1989.

Howe, Irving, and Kenneth Libo. *How We Lived: A Documentary History of Immigrant Jews in America, 1880–1930*. New York: Richard Marek Publishers, 1979.

Joseph, Morris. *Judaism as Creed and Life*. In *Essence of Judaism*, by Samuel Cohen. New York: Behrman's Jewish Book House, 1932.

Josephus, Flavius. *The Complete Works of Flavius Josephus*. Translated by William Whiston. Grand Rapids: Kregel, 1970.

Kafka, Franz. *Parables and Paradoxes*. New York: Schocken Books, 1958.

Kaye-Kantrowitz, Melanie, and Irena Kelpfisz, eds. *The Tribe of Dina: A Jewish Women's Anthology*. Boston: Beacon Press, 1986.

Kazin, Alfred. *A Walker in the City*. New York: Harcourt, Brace, Jovanovich, Inc., 1951, 1979.

Kishon, Ephraim. *Noah's Ark, Tourist Class*. Translated by Yohanan Goldman. Tel Aviv: N. Twersky Publishing House, Ltd., 1962.

Klagsbrun, Francine. *Voices of Wisdom: Jewish Ideals and Ethics for Everyday Living*. New York: Pantheon Books, 1980.

Kolatch, Alfred J. *Great Jewish Quotations*. New York: Jonathan David Publishers, Inc., 1996.

Kumove, Shirley. *Words Like Arrows: A Collection of Yiddish Folk Sayings*. New York: Schocken Books, 1985.

Kushner, Harold S. *When All You've Ever Wanted Isn't Enough*. New York: Pocket Books, 1986.

———. *To Life! A Celebration of Jewish Being and Thinking*. Boston: Warner Books, 1993.

Lamm, Maurice. *The Jewish Way in Death and Mourning*. New York: Jonathan David Publishers, Inc., 1969.

Lasher, Lawrence, ed. *Conversations with Bernard Malamud*. Jackson/London: University Press of Mississippi, 1991.

Lerman, Rhoda. *God's Ear*. New York: Henry Holt & Co., 1989.

Lester, Julius. *Lovesong: Becoming a Jew.* New York: Henry Holt & Co., 1988.

Levenson, Sam. *You Don't Have to Be in Who's Who to know What's What.* New York: Simon & Schuster, 1979.

Levi, Primo. *Survival in Auschwitz.* Translated from the Italian by Stuart Woolf. New York: Touchstone Books, 1958.

Maimonides, Moses. *The Code of Maimonides (Mishneh Torah).* Translated by the Yale Judaica Series. New Haven: Yale University Press, 1949–1972.

——. *The Preservation of Youth.* Translated by Hirsch L. Gordon. New York: Philosophical Library, Inc., 1958.

——. *The Guide of the Perplexed.* Translated with an introduction by Shlomo Pines. Chicago: University of Chicago Press, 1963.

Marx, Groucho. *Groucho and Me.* New York: Random House, Inc., 1959.

Millu, Liana. *Smoke over Birkenau.* Translated from the Italian by Lynne Sharon Schwartz. New York: Jewish Publication Society, 1991.

Morison, Walter, ed. and trans. *The Collected Stories of Isaac Babel.* New York: Penguin Group, 1955.

Moskowitz, Faye, ed. *Her Face in the Mirror: Jewish Women on Mothers and Daughters.* Boston: Beacon Press, 1994.

Nathan, Joan. *Jewish Cooking in America.* New York: Alfred A. Knopf, 1995.

Newman, Louis I. *The Hasidic Anthology: Tales and Teachings of the Hasidim.* New York: Bloch Publishing Co., 1944.

Olsen, Tillie. *Mother to Daughter, Daughter to Mother, Mothers on Mothering.* New York: Feminist Press, 1984.

Ovadyahu, Mordecai. *Bialik Speaks: Words from the Poet's Lips, Clues to the Man.* Translated by A. El-Dror. Ramat Gan, Israel: Massada Ltd. Press, 1969.

Paley, Grace. *The Collected Stories.* New York: Farrar Straus & Giroux, 1994.

Plimpton, George, ed. *Writers at Work: The Paris Review Interviews.* New York: The Viking Press, 1967.

Pogrebin Letty Cottin. *Deborah, Golda and Me.* New York: Crown Publishers, Inc., 1992.

——. *Getting Over Getting Older.* New York: Little, Brown & Company, 1996.

Proust, Marcel. *Remembrance of Things Past.* Translated by C. K. Montcrieff and Terence Kilmartin. New York: Random House, 1981.

Rittner, Carol, and John K. Roth, eds. *Different Voices: Women and the Holocaust.* New York: Paragon House, 1993.

Roden, Claudia. *The Book of Jewish Food: An Odyssey from Samarkand to New York.* New York: Alfred A. Knopf, 1996.

Rosten, Leo. *The Joys of Yiddish.* New York: Pocket Books, 1968.

———. *Treasury of Jewish Quotations.* New York: McGraw-Hill Book Co., 1972.

Rothchild, Sylvia. *Family Stories for Every Generation.* Detroit: Wayne State University Press, 1989.

Rubin, Steven J., ed. *Writing Our Lives: Autobiographies of American Jews, 1890–1990.* Philadelphia: The Jewish Publication Society, 1991.

Rukeyser, Muriel. *The Collected Poems, 1914–1980.* New York: McGraw-Hill, 1978.

Sachar, Abraham L. *A History of the Jews.* New York: Alfred A. Knopf, 1965.

Sachs, Nelly. *O the Chimneys.* Translated from the German by Michael Hamburger et al. New York: Farrar, Straus, 1967.

Schiff, Hilda, comp. *Holocaust Poetry.* New York: St. Martin's Press, 1995.

Schwartz, Howard, ed. *Gates to the New City: A Treasury of Modern Jewish Tales.* New York: Avon Books, 1983.

———. *Gabriel's Palace: Jewish Mystical Tales.* New York: Oxford University Press, 1993.

Schwartz, Howard, and Anthony Rudolf, eds. *Voices Within the Ark: The Modern Jewish Poets.* New York: Avon Books, 1980.

Schwartz, Leo W. *A Golden Treasury of Jewish Literature.* New York: Farrar & Rinehart, Inc., 1937.

———, ed. *The Jewish Caravan: Great Stories of 25 Centuries.* New York: Holt, Rinehart and Winston, 1965.

Schwartz, Richard H. *Judaism and Vegetarianism.* Marblehead, Mass.: Micah Publications, 1988.

Shahn, Ben. *The Shape of Content.* Cambridge: Harvard University Press, 1957.

Shenker, Israel. *Coat of Many Colors: Pages from Jewish Life.* Garden City, N.Y.: Doubleday & Co. Inc., 1985.

Shosteck, Patti. *A Lexicon of Jewish Cooking: A Collection of Folklore,*

Foodlore, History, Customs, and Recipes. Chicago: Contemporary Books, Inc., 1981.

Simon, Kate. *Bronx Primitive—Portraits in a Childhood.* New York: Harper Colophon Books, 1982.

Simon, Neil. *Rewrites.* New York: Simon & Schuster, 1996.

Slater, Elinor, and Robert Slater. *Great Jewish Women.* New York: Jonathan David Publishers, 1994.

Solotaroff, Ted, and Nessa Rapoport, eds. *Writing Our Way Home: Contemporary Stories by American Jewish Writers.* New York: Schocken Books, 1992.

Stein, David E., ed. *A Garden of Choice Fruit: 200 Classic Jewish Quotes on Human Beings and the Environment.* Wyncote, Pa.: Shomrei Adamah, 1991.

Steinsaltz, Adin. *The Essential Talmud.* Translated from the Hebrew by Chaya Galai. New York: BasicBooks, Inc., 1976.

———. *The Steinsaltz Talmud. Reference Guide and Selected Tractates.* New York: Random House, Inc., 1989.

Strassfeld, Michael. *The Jewish Holidays—A Guide and Commentary.* New York: Harper & Row Publishers, 1985.

Telushkin, Joseph. *Jewish Wisdom: Ethical, Spiritual, and Historical Lessons from the Great Works and Thinkers.* New York: William Morrow and Co., Inc., 1994.

Weiss, Rabbi Saul. *Insights: A Talmudic Treasury.* Jerusalem/New York: Feldheim Publishers, 1990.

Wiesel, Elie. *Gates of the Forest.* New York: Holt, Rinehart & Winston, 1966.

———. *Night.* New York: Hill and Wang, 1972.

———. *Sages and Dreamers: Biblical, Talmudic, and Hasidic Portraits and Legends.* New York: Summit Books, 1991.

Wolpe, David J. *Teaching Your Children About God.* New York: Henry Holt & Co., 1993.

Wouk, Herman, *This Is My God.* New York: Simon & Schuster, 1986.

Yezierska, Anzia. *The Breadgivers.* New York: Persea Books, Inc., 1975